I CAN
herringbone

Melissa Grakowsky

From Basic Stitch
to Advanced
Techniques,
a Comprehensive
Workbook for
Beaders

LARK CRAFTS
Asheville

EDITOR
Nathalie Mornu

TECHNICAL EDITOR
Rachel Nelson-Smith

EDITORIAL ASSISTANCE
Dawn Dillingham
Hannah Doyle
Abby Haffelt

ART DIRECTOR
Kathleen Holmes

JUNIOR DESIGNER
Carol Morse Barnao

ILLUSTRATORS
How to: Melissa Grakowsky
Difficulty levels: J'aime Allene

PHOTOGRAPHER
Lynne Harty

BOOK & COVER DESIGNER
Laura Palese

EDITORIAL INTERN
Alex Alesi

An Imprint of Sterling Publishing
387 Park Avenue South
New York, NY 10016

If you have questions or comments about
this book, please visit: larkcrafts.com

Library of Congress Cataloging-in-Publication Data

Grakowsky, Melissa.
  I CAN Herringbone : From Basic Stitch to Advanced Techniques, a
Comprehensive Workbook for Beaders / Melissa Grakowsky. -- First Edition.
     pages cm
  ISBN 978-1-4547-0362-4 (pbk.)
  1. Beadwork--Patterns. 2. Jewelry making. I. Title.
  TT860.G7325 2012
  745.594'2--dc23
                                      2012007122

10 9 8 7 6 5 4 3 2 1

First Edition

Published by Lark Crafts
An Imprint of Sterling Publishing Co., Inc.
387 Park Avenue South, New York, NY 10016

Text © 2012, Melissa Grakowsky
Photography © 2012, Lark Crafts, an Imprint of Sterling Publishing Co., Inc.,
unless otherwise specified
Illustrations © 2012, Melissa Grakowsky

Distributed in Canada by Sterling Publishing,
c/o Canadian Manda Group, 165 Dufferin Street
Toronto, Ontario, Canada M6K 3H6

Distributed in the United Kingdom by GMC Distribution Services,
Castle Place, 166 High Street, Lewes, East Sussex, England BN7 1XU

Distributed in Australia by Capricorn Link (Australia) Pty Ltd.,
P.O. Box 704, Windsor, NSW 2756 Australia

Manufactured in China

ISBN 13: 978-1-4547-0362-4

For information about custom editions, special sales, and premium and
corporate purchases, please contact the Sterling Special Sales Department at
800-805-5489 or specialsales@sterlingpub.com.

Submit requests for information about desk and examination copies available
to college and university professors to academic@larkbooks.com. Our complete policy can be found at www.larkcrafts.com.

contents

16   18   20   27

30   33   36

39   44   51

53   55   57

63   66   69   71

76   81   84

86   95   98

102   110   113

introduction

. . . .

I studied physics and painting in college. I think of science and artwork as very similar undertakings. You're given a set of techniques to use—I call these a "bag of tricks"—and when presented with a problem you have to pick from the bag to come up with a creative solution.

This method is exactly how I approach beading and why I like herringbone stitch so much! When I first envision a design, I have to pick from among my tricks to figure out how to create that design from the beads I have. Other times I play with beads that I like and use combinations of techniques just to experiment and see what the design possibilities are. Most of the time, my design process is a combination of these two practices. With this book, I hope to hand you some tricks to add to your bag.

When I first learned about herringbone stitch, I didn't want to use it. I was still in my peyote phase and was deeply immersed in exploring that stitch. When I finally succumbed to herringbone, I quickly realized that because of its tight structure, like peyote stitch, it afforded three-dimensional design possibilities.

Herringbone, at its most basic, is a pattern of parallel, nested zigzagging rows. This structure can be found in textiles, masonry, cross-stitch, basket weaving, and—most important for the purposes of this book—in off-loom beading.

Herringbone stitch is very versatile. It can be flat or tubular. It can be thick or thin. It can run a straight course, be curved, or even get formed into waves. You can bezel stones with it, create shapes, and combine it with other stitches to create entirely new ways of beading. I've crammed years of experimenting with herringbone into this book, and I think you'll be amazed by the variety of possibilities this stitch has to offer.

This book is a comprehensive guide to the stitch for beginners and advanced beaders alike, but let's start at the beginning. In chapter 1, I explain the essential materials and basic tools you'll need to get started. Chapter 2 provides the backbone of the entire book, teaching simple flat herringbone and introducing a few easy jewelry projects that teach the basic stitch. I don't tell you how to make them—instead, I *show* you, with plenty of illustrations every step of the way, in every project in the book, to help make sure you succeed.

Build on your knowledge in chapter 3 with interesting projects that show how to modify flat herringbone. The Poseidon's Gem Bracelet, for example, demonstrates how including different bead sizes can cause beadwork to curve, while the Earth Mother Earrings show how to make a disk.

Chapter 4 takes you to the next level with tubular herringbone. Chapter 5 teaches you to modify the tubular herringbone stitch in different ways to create a variety of results. The delicate Pod Earrings project shows how to add beads to widen a narrow tube, and with the extravagant Victorian Elegance Necklace you learn how to curve tubular herringbone, as well as decorate it with fringe.

Chapter 6 brings you the art of bezeled stones, with five projects detailing how to capture rivolis and cabochons in different ways.

You *can* herringbone! I hope you'll see this book not only as a guide to learning the stitch, but as a catalog of more advanced techniques that you'll reference for years to come, filled as it is with projects to inspire and plenty of tricks for your bag.

Examples of herringbone pattern

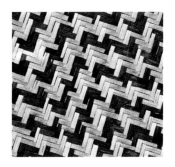

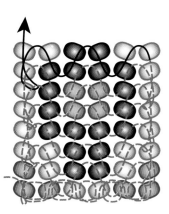

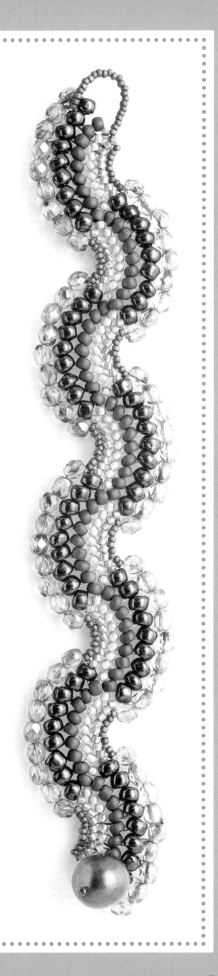

1

materials & tools

· ·

Herringbone experienced a re-emergence in the beading world toward the end of the 20th century, when several American beaders traveled to South Africa to study the beaded art of the Ndebele people, who have used the stitch extensively for centuries. Amazingly, their elaborate designs are created without the use of patterns or directions. The craft is passed down from generation to generation, and each piece of beadwork is a unique expression: In Ndebele jewelry, bead colors and patterns have specific meanings.

Creating patterns with different colored seed beads, the way the Ndebele do, is just the beginning. All sorts of materials are now available to beaders. By using different sizes and shapes of beads, you can add visual interest and stray from the paradigm of simple flat beadwork. Fair warning: Once you start beading, you may very well find yourself collecting more beads and tools than you ever meant to!

BEADS

There's an incredibly vast variety of beads to choose from—enough to write an encyclopedia cataloging all the options! In this section, I touch only on the types of beads used in this book, but keep in mind this is only the beginning.

Seed Beads

Seed beads are the basic material used in off-loom bead-weaving. They're made of glass, and quite tiny. You'll find them in a variety of sizes, denoted with a number followed by an ott symbol. Standard sizes range from 1° to 15°. The smaller the number, the larger the seed bead.

Manufactured mostly in the Czech Republic, Japan, and China, the seed beads from each region have subtle differences. Czech seed beads tend to be slightly rounder and smaller than Japanese and Chinese seed beads. Japanese and Chinese beads tend to be squarer, closer to a cylindrical shape. Many beaders prefer working with Japanese and Czech seed beads because they're generally more consistent in size, shape, and color than their Chinese counterparts.

As mentioned above, Czech seed beads are slightly smaller than their Japanese or Chinese counterparts. This difference is most apparent in the smallest of sizes. Size 15° Czech beads are *much* smaller than 15° Japanese seed beads, whereas 11° Czech seed beads are very close in size to 11° Japanese seed beads.

> **TIP:** For many bead projects, including the ones in this book, you can use any type of seed bead in the sizes specified, with the exception of beads 12° and smaller. For these, it's essential to use the beads from the country of origin specified in order to get the desired outcome.

In general, the term **seed bead** means a round bead shaped like a small seed, or a **rocaille**. However, many different seed beads don't necessarily have a round shape.

Cylinder beads are one of the most popular seed bead shapes after rocailles. They have thinner walls equidistant from the center of the bead on all sides. Their uniformity and square shape allow beaders to use these beads as building blocks for many different projects that require structure and precision.

Another popular seed bead shape is the **drop.** The holes of drops are closer to one side of the bead. Drops vary in shape depending on the manufacturer, size, and brand of bead.

Another popular type has cuts or facets on the surface—anywhere from one to six facets, cut at regular intervals or randomly. **Hex beads** have six even facets cut around the widest point of the bead. **Charlottes** have one to three small facets cut at random places on their surfaces. **Cut cylinder beads** have even facets around the midline.

In addition to these popular types, there are many other types of seed beads, including, but not limited to, **peanut beads, triangles,** and **squares.**

Finishes

The limitless number of colors and finishes from which to choose can be delightfully overwhelming. Manufacturers often catalog their seed beads first by size and then by finish type, with a variety of colors in each finish category. Multiple types of finishes can be applied to the same base bead, so each category contains all the beads with the specified finish or finishes applied to them. Beads are colored and finished in batches, called dye lots, so it's possible to find beads that have the same color number but look subtly different. Below, I describe the main categories of finishes.

Metallic beads come in standard metallic colors like gold, copper, and silver, as well as metallic versions of dozens of hues, in tones from pastel to bold and bright.

Transparent beads conduct light—as opposed to solidly colored **opaque** beads through which light may not pass. Both types come in a rainbow of color possibilities.

Lined beads are made of colored translucent glass lined with a color in the bead hole. There are many combinations of glass color and lining color, including beads that are silver-lined, gold-lined, copper-lined, brass-lined, and color-lined with a wide palette of choices of glass color.

A final category, which usually doesn't come with any type of finish applied, is **silk** or **satin** beads. These have a fiber optic effect, so they transmit light very differently from other types of seed beads. They resemble tiger's-eye in the way they catch and reflect light.

With the exception of silk or satin beads, seed beads can all have different finishes, which are treatments applied to the base color of bead to add another layer of variety and visual interest. **Matte** finishes are applied to the types of beads listed above, with different results. Matte transparent beads look reminiscent of beach glass, while matte metallic beads have a very antique feel. Matte opaque beads are a great option when you need color but want to limit the eye-catching sparkle of a piece. **Luster** finishes are very shiny final coatings of beads and sometimes come in a different color hue than the base bead color. **Ceylon** beads have a pearl-like effect. The result is a very shiny bead that reflects light in a similar manner to a pearl.

Another finish goes under different names when applied to different types of beads and produced by different manufacturers. It's most often referred to as **rainbow**, **aurora borealis (AB)**, or **iris**. This is essentially an iridescent effect that creates multiple hues on the surface of the bead. The beads retain their overall color but reflect a rainbow of shades. This is extremely interesting and beautiful when used properly in beadwork.

Glass Beads

This category encompasses all glass beads other than seed beads. Don't confuse Czech **fire-polished** beads with regular Czech glass beads. During manufacture, fire-polished beads are first faceted, then heated to soften the facets. This results in a unique, shiny look when the finish is applied. These beads are more limited in shape than regular Czech glass beads. Many beaders prefer the round fire-polished shape, elongated slightly in the direction of the bead hole. Because they're not truly spherical, take into consideration the shape of these beads when using them in a three-dimensional piece of beadwork. Like seed beads, these come in a variety of colors and finishes.

Because of their small size, **bugle** beads could arguably be included in the seed bead category. Czech and Japanese manufacturers make these elongated cylindrical beads, which are available in a variety of colors and finishes. They come in sizes from micro bugles— which measure about 2 mm, with holes comparable to those of Czech 15° seed beads—to 35-mm bugles, a vintage size not widely produced. The more common sizes are #1 through #5, with the smaller number denoting a smaller bead, and 12 mm. Although Czech and Japanese bugles both use the same numbering system, their sizes actually differ.

Pearls

Pearls are similar to shell beads in their natural luminescence. Although you can find both saltwater and freshwater pearls, freshwater are more common. These are often actually plastic beads placed inside mollusks to be surface-coated with nacre (the pearl material). This makes them less costly; genuine, 100 percent natural pearls are incredibly expensive and mainly used by the fine jewelry industry.

Dyed pearls are common, and the color range is surprisingly vast. Be careful when you purchase: one batch dyed a particular color may not exactly match the next batch of pearls dyed the same color.

Gemstone Beads

Sprinkled in these projects are coin, briolette, and faceted rondelle shapes made from minerals cut to shape and then polished, either by hand or produced in a factory. That's a mere sampling of what's available. This category includes precious gemstones such as sapphire and ruby, as well as semiprecious gemstones like amazonite.

Crystals

Almost nothing else sparkles like faceted crystal. Crystal is just glass with certain heavy metals infused into its molecular structure, so the glass captures and reflects light with more intensity.

The three main countries manufacturing crystal beads are China, the Czech Republic, and Austria. As with seed beads, different colors and finishes combine to produce various beautiful effects. One finish, aurora borealis (AB), gives the surface a rainbow color effect while allowing the base color to shine through. Some of the most popular shapes used in beaded jewelry are bicones, rounds, and rondelles, but there are many more to choose from.

Austrian manufacturers have developed a process that applies two coats of AB finish to the beads, which creates a more opaque rainbow effect on the surface and changes the appearance much more. Sometimes it's hard to tell what the original base color of these extremely popular double AB (2XAB) coated beads is because the double AB coating tends to look very blue/green.

Glass Cabochons and Crystal Stones

These focal jewelry components do not contain holes, so it's necessary to create *bezels* to incorporate them into jewelry. Cabochons have a smooth, rounded face and a flat back, while all other stones have rounded, faceted, or pointed backs. These components come in a variety of shapes, including oval, round, and square, along with many others.

Stones made of crystal, glass, and plastic tantalize us with unlimited possibility—as do their gemstone counterparts. The diversity of color, shape, pattern, and finish is staggering.

THREAD

The two basic categories are braided and non-braided threads.

Non-Braided Threads

This category of multiple fibers twisted together includes all the types of nylon thread as well as natural threads like silk. Some popular brands are Nymo, Silamide, and Toho One-G. Non-braided threads are supple and prone to stretching over time. In fact, it's good practice to stretch them before beginning a project so they'll stretch less in the finished project, which will then be less likely to lose its shape.

The supple quality of non-braided thread gives finished beadwork a softer feel than if it were stitched with braided thread. For many projects, this is desirable. Non-braided threads come in a variety of thicknesses. Some projects may require thicker thread to hold larger beads in place or create more structure, while other projects may require thinner threads that pass through smaller beads multiple times.

Non-braided threads have a tendency to knot. Limit this by working with a wingspan, at most, of thread. Ironing or steaming can help prevent knots by straightening the individual fibers, but because each thread is different,

this might work better with some threads than with others. Toho One-G thread, which comes off the spool in a corkscrew shape, responds well to this. With other brands, it's unnecessary. Mitigate fraying by coating the thread with synthetic wax or beeswax. Another way to combat fraying is to work with shorter lengths of thread, and make a habit of weaving in old thread before starting a new one.

Braided Threads

These recent arrivals in the beading world include WildFire and FireLine, which are actually fishing line! They consist of thinner threads braided together and coated with polymer for a smooth surface; this structure makes them especially strong and resistant to fraying, and therefore perfect for working with heavy beads, crystal, and metal beads that have sharp edges. However, this positive quality actually has a negative impact on one of your primary beading tools—it dulls scissors!

Braided beading threads come in different pounds of strength. They stretch slightly over time, but much less so than non-braided threads. They're also considerably stiffer than non-braided threads, so they lend heft and rigidity to beadwork. If your beading project is structural and needs stiffness to be successful, this type of thread is a good choice.

Thread Color

There's no right or wrong choice. For most projects, thread is merely a material that holds the beadwork together and not something that you want attracting a lot of attention. The best way to prevent non-braided thread from looking prominent is to choose a color close to the dominant bead color. Sometimes, though, beaders want to emphasize the thread, so they choose a dominant color that stands out against the beads.

The color range of braided thread is limited. You might wish to color light shades of braided thread with permanent marker to match it to the beads in the project.

FINDINGS AND COMPONENTS

These little jewelry parts, usually made from metal, are essential building blocks in the creation of functional, wearable beaded artwork. Components come in a variety of finishes. They can be plain or embellished.

Commercially made **clasps** come in a wide variety of styles, including, but not limited to, lobster clasps, toggles and rings, pinch clasps, barrel clasps, magnetic clasps, and s-hook clasps. Some jewelry pieces look better with handmade, beaded clasps, but for simpler projects, commercial clasps are often a sensible choice.

Buttons with shanks or holes have found their way from apparel to jewelry making. Placed opposite a loop of strung seed beads, buttons with shanks are a quick way to create a closure on a necklace or bracelet.

Ear wires are metal components designed to hang comfortably from pierced ears. Finish options include gold, silver, brass, and other metallic hues, in a vast array of styles from which to choose. Some have a lever back or other means of closing to prevent the ear wire from falling out of the ear; others have embellishments or elaborate designs. All of the varieties have a small loop of wire at the bottom or another means of attaching beads and other jewelry components. For unpierced ears, there are also clip-on earring components to which you can attach beads the same way.

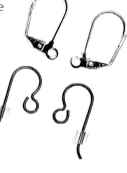

TOOLS

You really don't need many tools to get started.

Needles

The eye of a beading needle is about the same width as the shaft, so it can easily go through the small holes in seed beads without sticking. This brilliant and necessary feature also makes beading needles somewhat tricky to thread. Here are some tips: rather than threading the needle, *needle the thread* as follows. Hold the end of the thread so the tip just emerges from between your two fingers. Push the eye of the needle down onto the tiny end of thread. Your fingers help keep the thread from bending while the eye is forced to come down around the thread. Moistening the thread or using beading wax on the end can help.

Beading needles range in size from 9 to 15; the smaller the number, the larger the needle size. For seed beads, use size 10 to 13. Size 12 needles are a very good all-purpose size, but when I stitch through 15°s multiple times I like to have size 13s on hand just in case any of the beads have slightly smaller holes and the size 12 needle gets stuck.

All needles meet their end by either breaking or because the eye becomes smaller and smaller from being forced through beads so many times. It's normal to need more than one needle to complete a single project, so make sure you have extra needles on hand!

Scissors
For most projects, any type of craft scissors is sufficient. Seasoned beaders, however, like to keep a pair of small, very sharp scissors in their beading kit. Use them to cut a point into the beading thread so it's easier to thread and to trim the ending thread very close to the beadwork so it won't show. Braided thread is so strong it will dull the scissors, so reserve a pair for only this type of thread.

Thread Burner
When you activate this pen-size, battery-operated device, a small coil of wire on its tip heats up enough to burn through any type of thread. This tool is great for times where you need to trim thread close to the surface in an area you can't reach with scissors.

Chain-Nose Pliers
If your project requires multiple passes of thread through the same bead, the needle may eventually get stuck in the hole and you'll have to grip it with pliers to pull it completely through. This can be risky because you could break the bead from the inside out. You'll learn to feel the subtle difference between a stuck needle that will break a bead if you try to force it through and a needle that just needs some extra help.

Pliers are also useful for straightening out needles. Finally, they're the tool to grab when you notice, several rows after the fact, that you accidentally incorporated extra beads into the beadwork—this really does happen! Just pinch and crush the bead to break it instead of pulling out your beadwork up to the point of the mistake. This method isn't necessarily desirable because broken glass around the thread can wreck its integrity. Placing a needle through the bead as you break it reduces the chances of the thread being cut, though it guarantees nothing.

Beading Awl
Beading awls are by no means necessary, but they're useful for pulling out thread from beadwork, which is necessary from time to time. You could do this with a needle, but needles often break or bend.

Like pliers, awls are also useful in breaking unwanted beads that have accidentally made their way into your beadwork. Break the bead from the inside out by pushing the awl into the bead hole while holding the beadwork against a hard surface. This method is less likely to harm the thread.

Beading Surface
Many different types of commercial beading surfaces are available, some with built-in storage designed for travel. However, you can easily make one of the best surfaces by cutting a small rectangle from an old Vellux blanket. (You can also purchase a Vellux mat in a bead shop.) The fibers of Vellux prevent seed beads from rolling around easily.

flat herringbone stitch

Flat herringbone stitch uses beads in a way that creates a
two-dimensional fabric. It looks beautiful plain, with color
patterns, or as a base for embellishment, and you can vary
the width of the stitch.

ABOUT ILLUSTRATIONS

As shown in figure 1, the working thread
path for the step described is drawn in black,
with the needle end of the thread shown
with an arrow. When shown, dashed gray
lines represent thread paths from previous
steps. For precision, thread paths from tricky
maneuvers are shown in red.

FIGURE I

Thread from previous step

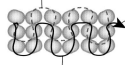

Needle
direction

Working thread

LADDER STITCH

Ladder stitch is a companion stitch to herringbone. Use it to start a base of beads that becomes the first row of the project. *Note:* To add stability to a ladder, you may repeat each stitch before moving to the next one.

Thread your needle—or, needle your thread—with about 18 inches (45.7 cm) of thread. This is a good working length for a small sample project. Holding the needle in your dominant hand and the tail thread in your other hand, pick up two seed beads and slide them toward the end of the thread until they're about 4 inches (10.2 cm) from the end. Continue holding the thread so the beads don't fall off.

Stitch through the first bead you picked up, from the tail side of the thread toward the needle side. Take out any slack in the thread. The two beads should appear to sit side by side, with their bead holes parallel (figure 2).

Stitch through the second bead from the side of the bead your needle is closest to (figure 3).

Use this two-bead base for single-ladder flat herringbone stitch (shown in the next section), or you can continue to ladder additional beads, one at a time, until you have a base large enough for the number of ladders in your project.

Pick up a third bead. Stitch through the second bead again, then through the third bead. Pull the thread to take out any slack (figure 4). You now have three beads laddered together. Add a fourth bead the same way you added the third. You now have a base of four beads that would be suitable to start a two-ladder flat herringbone project. This laddered base counts as row 1 (figure 5).

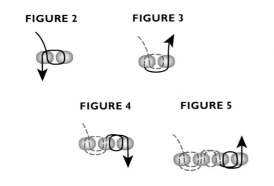

FIGURE 2   **FIGURE 3**

FIGURE 4   **FIGURE 5**

You may have noticed that each time you add another bead, your thread ends up on the opposite side of the laddered row; that's the nature of ladder stitch.

TERMINOLOGY

ladder (*noun*): A stack of bead pairs to which you add additional pairs of beads during each stitch. (*verb*): To use ladder stitch.

needle up: Thread the needle with a length of cut thread.

pick up: Pick up beads with your needle, or push the beads onto your needle.

step up (*noun*): The act of stepping up. (*verb*): To stitch through either the first or the last bead in the row—depending on the particular stitch used—to position your thread to start the next row.

stitch (*noun*): Each act of adding a bead or beads to the needle, then pushing the needle through a bead or beads. (*verb*): To push the needle through a bead hole or multiple bead holes.

stitch back through: Stitch through the bead—or beads—specified in the reverse direction from which you last stitched.

stitch through again: Stitch through the bead—or beads—specified in the same direction you last stitched.

tail: The end of the thread, opposite the needle.

tension: The force with which you pull on the needle end of the thread when stitching. Higher tension creates stiffer beadwork and lower tension creates more supple beadwork.

weave in: Weave your thread into the beadwork following previous thread paths between beads, so the thread doesn't show.

wingspan: A length of thread that reaches from one hand to the other when you hold your arms completely outstretched.

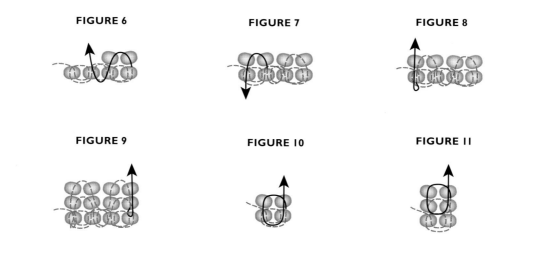

FIGURE 6   FIGURE 7   FIGURE 8

FIGURE 9   FIGURE 10   FIGURE 11

TWO-LADDER FLAT HERRINGBONE STITCH

To start a two-ladder flat herringbone project from off the four-bead laddered base, pick up the first pair of beads specified by the project. Stitch down through the bead in the base adjacent to the one from which your thread is emerging. Then stitch up through the next bead in the base (figure 6).

Pick up the next pair of beads and stitch down through the next bead in the base (figure 7).

Because this is the last pair of beads in the row, you'll need to do a *turn-around* and *step up* to start the next row. Catch a loop of thread close to where your thread is emerging by stitching underneath or around it. Then stitch back through the last bead stitched through and the last bead added (figure 8).

You've completed row 2 and your thread is now in position to start row 3. Work row 3 in exactly the same manner as row 2 but in the opposite direction. Work all the subsequent rows in the same fashion as well. Work even-count rows in the opposite direction of odd-count rows in multiple-ladder flat herringbone stitch (figure 9). (In single-ladder flat herringbone stitch, this does not occur.)

SINGLE-LADDER FLAT HERRINGBONE STITCH

Start with a base of two beads, which you've laddered together, as shown in figure 2. For row 2, pick up the next bead pair, then stitch down through the adjacent bead in the base. Stitch up through the first bead in the base and the bead after that to step up and prepare for the next row. Because there's only one ladder, each row is only one stitch, and each stitch includes the step up to the next row (figure 10).

Add each subsequent row in exactly the same way as row 2 (figure 11).

MULTIPLE-LADDER FLAT HERRINGBONE STITCH

You can do flat herringbone stitch with any number of ladders. Some projects, like Starry Night Necklace (page 39), require a large number of ladders. In this case, the first row spans the entire length of the necklace, and you work in a direction perpendicular to most of the other projects. Other projects use only one, two, or three ladders. Regardless, the technique is the same: you start with a laddered base, then work each row pair by pair, and end each row with a step up to get ready for the next row.

STARTING AND STOPPING THREAD

Whenever you start a project, leave a 4-inch (10.2 cm) tail thread hanging. While you work, grip this tail thread with your nondominant hand by wrapping the thread around a finger until you have a few rows of beadwork established and the stitched beads are in place. This ensures you won't lose any beads.

Pay careful attention to the directions; they'll indicate whether you need to leave a slightly longer tail to use as a working thread later. Depending on the project, you may or may not need to use the tail thread to add more beads from that end of the thread. Once you've established a few rows of beadwork and if you don't need the tail thread, secure it into the beadwork and trim it.

FIGURE 12

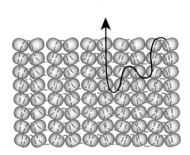

FIGURE 13

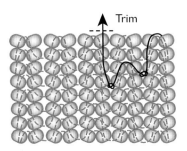

In most projects, you may run out of thread before finishing the project. When the working thread is shorter than 6 inches (15.2 cm), it becomes tricky to maneuver. Stop beading and weave your working thread into the beadwork, making sure it's secure and won't pull out of the beadwork, causing beads to fall off!

To do this, weave through the beadwork, following previous thread paths between beads and changing direction at least three times. Changing direction multiple times creates enough friction on the thread that it won't loosen (figure 12). You should follow thread paths that already exist between beads to avoid creating any new tension between beads and thus changing the movement between the two beads. If you add a thread path where one doesn't already exist, it will be apparent in your finished beadwork because the beads will curve in the wrong direction or pull too close together. This technique takes some practice to get used to, but once you learn how to move from bead to bead following old thread paths, you'll be able to secure your threads without even thinking.

An alternative to weaving in is knotting the working thread to previous thread between beads, though this technique works best in combination with reversing direction, because knots alone can sometimes come untied.

Once the thread is secure, trim it as close to the beadwork as possible by holding the thread in your hand, letting the beadwork hang, and pushing sharp scissors or a thread-burning tool down against the beadwork as you cut or burn the thread (figure 13).

After securing your old working thread, to continue working you must add a new length of thread. This is a similar process to securing threads but in reverse order. Needle up your new thread, then stitch through a few beads in the project close to where you left off, leaving at least a 1-inch (2.5 cm) tail sticking out of the beadwork, which you can trim later. Secure your new thread in the beadwork by weaving around and reversing direction, by knotting, or by a combination of the two. Once the thread is secure, weave to the point you left off in the project, making sure the orientation of your thread as it exits the last bead is correct (figure 14). Then trim your tail thread and begin stitching again!

FIGURE 14

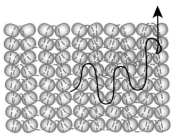

hodgepodge bracelet

Try making this bracelet as an easy project to practice herringbone stitch. Select a toggle that matches your bead colors, and begin!

YOU'LL NEED

3 colors of the same size seed bead (15°s, 8°s, 11°s, or even 6°s):

A, 4 g

B, 7 g

C, 7 g

Clasp or button

Size 12 and 13 beading needles

Black beading thread

Scissors

Work surface

TECHNIQUES

Ladder Stitch

Flat Herringbone Stitch

DIMENSIONS

6¾ inches (17.1 cm) long

DIFFICULTY LEVEL

Easy beginner

1 Needle up a wingspan of thread. Leaving a 12-inch (30.5 cm) tail, ladder together the following beads: A, A, B, B, A, A.

Row 2: Stitch one A and one B onto ladder 1. Stitch two Cs onto ladder 2. Stitch one B and one A onto ladder 3.

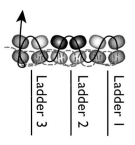

Row 3: Stitch two Bs onto ladder 3. Stitch two Cs onto ladder 2. Stitch two Bs onto ladder 1.

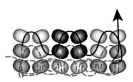

Row 4: Stitch one B and one C onto ladder 1. Stitch two Cs onto ladder 2. Stitch one C and one B onto ladder 3.

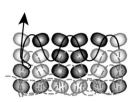

Row 5: Stitch one B and one C onto ladder 3. Stitch two As onto ladder 2. Stitch one C and one B onto ladder 1.

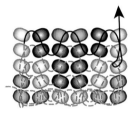

Row 6: Repeat row 5.

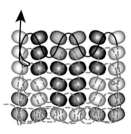

Row 7: Repeat row 4.

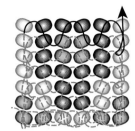

Row 8: Repeat row 3.

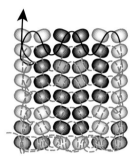

Row 9: Repeat row 2.

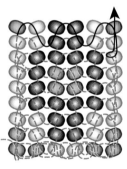

Row 10: Stitch two As onto ladder 1. Stitch two Bs onto ladder 2. Stitch two Cs onto ladder 3.

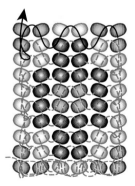

2 Repeat rows 1 through 10 until your bracelet is the desired length, leaving room for whichever clasp type you choose. For example, if you're adding a toggle and ring clasp that measures ¾ inch (1.9 cm) in length when closed, stitch your bracelet until it's ¾ inch (1.9 cm) short of the desired length.

3 To add the clasp, reverse direction and stitch through the last bead you exited, then reverse direction and stitch out through the adjacent bead. Pick up two of the same color bead, the small loop on the clasp, and two matching beads. Stitch into the first bead in the end row of ladder 3, then the first bead in the next row of ladder 3. Catch a loop of thread, then reverse direction and stitch back through all of the beads added.

Repeat the thread path with as many passes of thread as the bead holes will allow, then secure your thread in the beadwork and trim it.

4 Needle up your tail thread. Add the other half of the clasp in the same manner as adding the loop. If you are using a button instead of a clasp, add enough beads to create a loop that will fit around your button to fasten. Secure your thread in the beadwork and trim it.

quartets bracelet

You can vary the appearance of flat herringbone stitch by mixing different beads. Here, a combination of seed beads and Czech fire-polished beads results in a fun, chunky bracelet, and a pretty ribbon closure keeps it romantic. Try experimenting with colors for different looks.

YOU'LL NEED

Size 8° silk metallic silver round seed beads, 7 g

176 crystal fire-polished rounds, 3 mm

18 inches (45.7 cm) of light gray polyester ribbon, ¾ inch (1.9 cm) wide

Size 12 beading needles

Gray beading thread

Scissors

Work surface

TECHNIQUE

Flat Herringbone Stitch

DIMENSIONS

7 inches (17.8 cm) long

DIFFICULTY LEVEL

Easy beginner

OVERVIEW

You'll start this bracelet by laddering together the first row of beads, then use that row as a base to build the rest of the bracelet in flat herringbone stitch. Add one type of bead in each row, which varies from row to row.

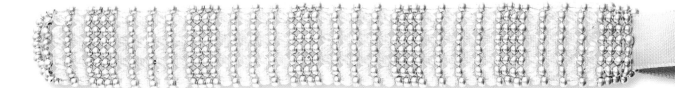

1 Needle up a wingspan of thread. Leaving an 18-inch (45.7 cm) tail, ladder together eight 8°s to create a base.

2 Add one row of 8°s in flat herringbone stitch. At the end of the row, catch a thread on the underside of row 1 and bring your thread out of the last bead added to step up.

Row 2–4: Add 8°s for these rows.
Row 5: Add fire-polished beads.
Row 6: Add 8°s.
Row 7: Add fire-polished beads.
Row 8: Add 8°s.
Row 9: Add fire-polished beads.
Row 10: Add 8°s.
Row 11: Add fire-polished beads.

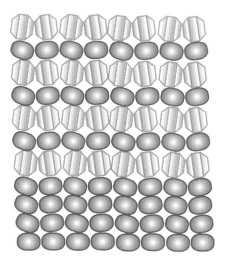

Repeat rows 1 through 11 until your bracelet is ½ inch (1.3 cm) shy of the desired finished length. The ribbon closure will add an adjustable amount of length to your bracelet—a minimum of ½ inch (1.3 cm).

CLOSURE

After finishing the last row, pick up ten 8°s and stitch down through the bead on the other end of the end row. Catch a thread and reverse direction so you can stitch through the loop of 8°s again to reinforce.

Repeat the thread path through the loop at least once more, then secure your thread in the beadwork and trim it.

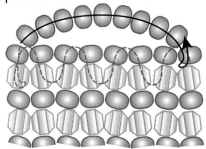

Needle up the tail thread and create the same loop on the other end of the bracelet. Then secure your thread in the beadwork and trim it.

To close the bracelet, thread one end of the ribbon through one loop on the end of the bracelet and the other end of ribbon through the other loop. Put the bracelet on your wrist and let out or take up slack and tie a bow when your bracelet fits.

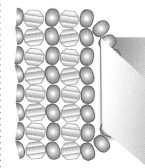
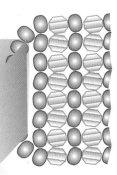

center of gravity earrings

These earrings made with flat herringbone stitch are simple enough to complete in about an hour!

YOU'LL NEED

Size 11° round seed beads:

A, gold-lined aqua, 1 g

B, matte stabilized galvanized silver, 1 g

C, silk silver, 1 g

20 aqua/celadon crystal bicones, 3 mm

4 aqua/celadon crystal bicones, 4 mm

Size 15° gold-lined aqua round seed beads, 1 g

28 celadon crystal bicones, 3 mm

4 celadon crystal bicones, 4 mm

8 light gray glass pearls, 6 mm

2 sterling silver ear wires

Size 12 and 13 beading needles*

Gray beading thread

Scissors

Work surface

*You'll bead this project with size 12 needles, but keep size 13s on hand in case small holes, like those in the gold-lined 15° beads, cause you problems.

TECHNIQUES

Flat Herringbone Stitch

Fringing

DIMENSIONS

2½ inches (6.4 cm) long

DIFFICULTY LEVEL

Experienced beginner

OVERVIEW

You'll create the base of the earring in flat herringbone stitch. After adding a fringe of crystals and pearls, you'll add the ear wire and one final detail embellishment at the top of the earring.

BASE

Needle up 1 yard (91.4 cm) of thread. Ladder together the following beads to form your first row: A, B, C, C, B, and A. Leave just enough of a tail to weave into the beadwork later and trim.

Stitch a second row in flat herringbone stitch, adding beads of the same color atop the beads in the first row. At the end of the row, catch a thread loop on the underside of row 1, then bring your thread out of the last bead added.

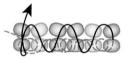

Stitch six more rows identical to the second row for a total of eight rows.

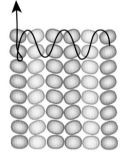

FRINGE

Fringe 1: Pick up five 3-mm aqua/celadon bicones, one 4-mm aqua/celadon bicone, and one 15°. Skip the 15° and stitch back through the rest of the beads you just picked up. Stitch into the A in the base, then out through the adjacent B.

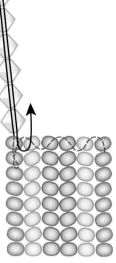

Fringe 2: Pick up seven 3-mm celadon bicones, one 4-mm celadon bicone, and one 15°. Skip the 15° and stitch back through the rest of the beads you just picked up. Stitch into the B in the base, then out through the adjacent C.

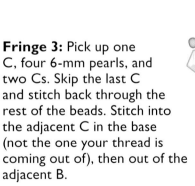

Fringe 3: Pick up one C, four 6-mm pearls, and two Cs. Skip the last C and stitch back through the rest of the beads. Stitch into the adjacent C in the base (not the one your thread is coming out of), then out of the adjacent B.

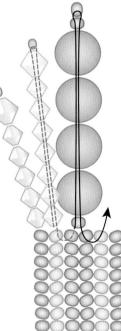

Fringe 4: Repeat fringe 2, stitching back into the B in the base, then out the adjacent A.

Fringe 5: Repeat fringe 1. Then stitch through the entire column of A on the edge of the base.

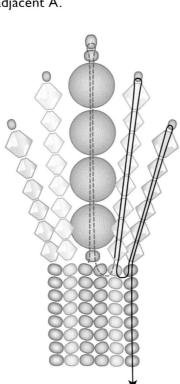

EAR WIRE AND FINISHING
Pick up twenty 15°s and the bottom ear wire loop. Stitch into the top A on the opposite side of the earring base, catch a loop of thread, and stitch back through the loop of 15°s, then into the A in the base and the next A in the same column of beads. Stitch up through the adjacent B, then out through the nearest C.

Pick up three Cs and stitch down through the adjacent Cs in the base. Weave your thread into the beadwork and secure it, then trim it.

Weave your tail thread into the earring base and trim it. Repeat all steps to make a second earring.

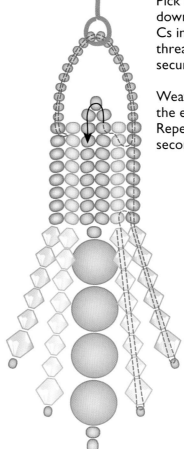

3

variations of flat herringbone stitch

In this chapter, I hope to give you a good idea of how easy it is to modify herringbone stitch. When you combine the techniques below with beads of different color and size, you have virtually limitless possibilities for flat herringbone stitch designs. Trying new combinations is the most exciting part of beading. The only limit is your imagination!

FIGURE 1

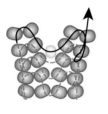

FIGURE 2

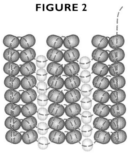

FIGURE 3

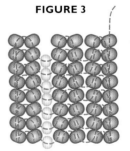

ADDING BEADS BETWEEN LADDERS

This variation is all about forcing ladders apart by adding beads between them, like in Lacy Wrap Choker. To do this, add the normal pair of beads to the ladder you're working on, then stitch down through the adjacent bead. Before you stitch up through the first bead in the next ladder, pick up the bead you want showing up between ladders. Then stitch up through two rows of beads in the next ladder, and add the next pair of beads in the basic technique (figure 1).

Another option is to add the same size bead between multiple ladders along the entire length of the project (figure 2).

In figure 3, there are added beads between some ladders and not others.

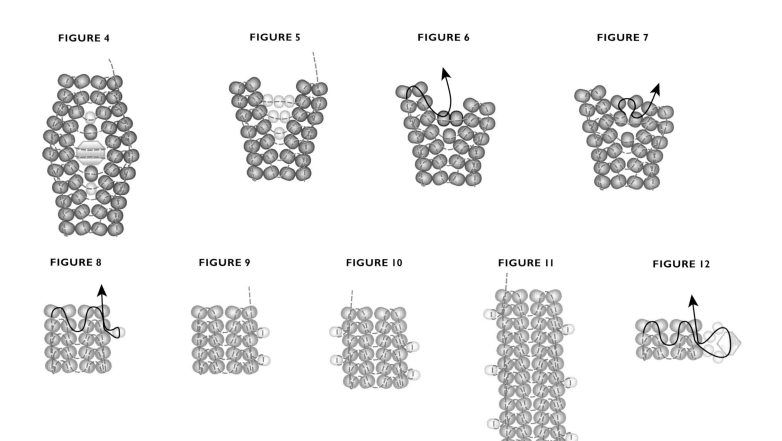

FIGURE 4   **FIGURE 5**   **FIGURE 6**   **FIGURE 7**

FIGURE 8   **FIGURE 9**   **FIGURE 10**   **FIGURE 11**   **FIGURE 12**

Also try adding beads of different sizes between ladders. Doing this forces the two ladders to move farther apart where the larger beads are present and closer together where the smaller beads or no beads are present (figure 4).

You can also add multiple beads at a time between ladders (figure 5). Adding an increasing number of beads between ladders will spread the ladders farther away from each other only to a point. After that point, which varies by bead type and size, the extra beads between ladders will only start to fold up on each other.

If you add a pair of beads between ladders, you can use that pair of beads to start a new ladder. Once the pair of beads is in place and you start the next row, add pairs of beads normally until you get to the bead pair. Stitch through only one of the beads in the pair (figure 6).

Pick up a pair of beads and stitch down through the next, and then up through the first bead in the next ladder. The pair of beads you just added between the ladders has turned into the second row of the new ladder (figure 7).

ADDING BEADS TO THE OUTSIDE OF LADDERS

You can also add beads on the outsides of ladders to break up the straight outline of flat herringbone, as seen in Lacy Wrap Choker.

First, stitch a row normally. When you get to the end of the row, and before you catch a thread and turn around to step up, pick up a bead and reverse direction, stitching back through the last two beads to step up. The bead you added on the outside of the ladder eliminates the step where you catch a bead thread in order to turn around (figure 8).

You can add outer beads on only one side of the ladders (figure 9), or you can add beads on both sides (figure 10). You'll notice that when you add beads to the outside of one ladder, they appear between every other row or seem to be alternating. Add beads when you do the turn-around in that ladder, which only happens on the same side of the herringbone every other row—not every row.

Another way to vary this form of embellishment is by adding beads every other row, rather than every row. This spaces out the embellishment beads more (figure 11).

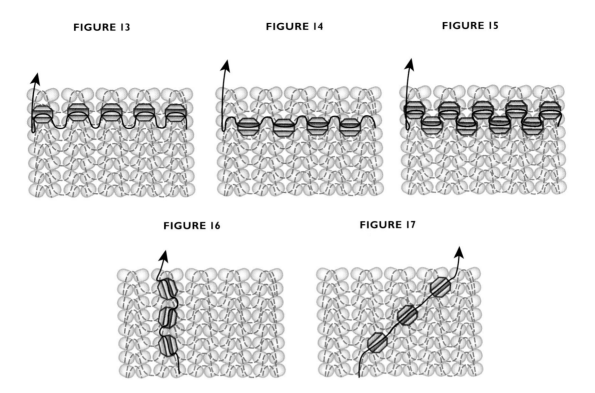

FIGURE 13   FIGURE 14   FIGURE 15

FIGURE 16   FIGURE 17

Or try adding multiple beads on the outside of a ladder and beads of different sizes (figure 12).

EMBELLISHMENTS

Two-Ladder Tennis Bracelet and Starry Night Necklace show ways to add embellishments to the surface of flat herringbone stitch to dress up a piece and create another layer of visual interest. You can add any of the variations described below to herringbone at least two ladders wide—even to unembellished projects in this book!

Add embellishment between bead pairs in each ladder (figure 13), between ladders (figure 14), or both at the same time (figure 15).

Add embellishment beads along the length of a ladder as you weave back and forth between the two sides of the ladder (figure 16).

Another option is to add embellishments along a diagonal, stitching between beads on side 1 of the first ladder, then side 2 of the second ladder, etc. (figure 17).

VARYING BEAD SIZES

Bend herringbone to your will by varying the size of beads used within the weave. Adding larger sizes of beads next to smaller ones causes the beadwork to change shape. The larger beads take up more space than the smaller beads, and the thread holds all of the beads together so they remain touching. As a result, you create either a curved flat piece of herringbone—such as Poseidon's Gem Bracelet or a three-dimensional piece of herringbone like Sinusoidal Necklace.

Adding larger beads to one side of a single ladder of flat herringbone pushes the smaller beads to one side and the ladder begins to curve. This happens because the larger beads stacked on top of one another have

FIGURE 18

a greater length than the stack of smaller beads. Because the outside of a curve is longer than the inside, after several rows the beadwork naturally takes on a curved shape in one direction, while remaining flat (figure 18).

You can create the same effect with multiple ladders by using several different sizes of beads. In order to get a flat curve, use the largest beads on the outside of the curve and the smallest beads on the inside, with intermittent sizes in between. For example, if you want to achieve a

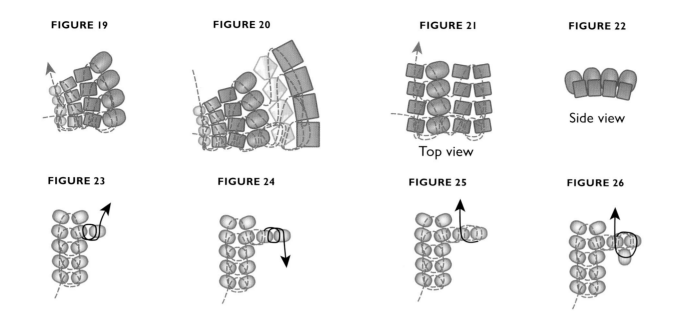

FIGURE 19

FIGURE 20

FIGURE 21

FIGURE 22

Side view

Top view

FIGURE 23

FIGURE 24

FIGURE 25

FIGURE 26

two-dimensional, flat curve with two ladders, you can use 15°s and 11° cylinder beads on ladder 1, and 10° cylinder beads and 8°s on ladder 2, respectively. This combination of beads works because 15°s are smaller than 11° cylinders, which are smaller than 10° cylinders, which are smaller than 8°s (figure 19).

If you want to get a comparable flat curve with three ladders, you can use 15°s and 11° cylinders on ladder 1, 10° cylinders and 8°s on ladder 2, and 3-mm bicones and 4-mm cubes on ladder 3 (figure 20). The size difference of these beads is proportionally correct to give you a flat piece of herringbone. If you use beads that are different in size, but not quite in the correct ratio, your stitching may start to curve into the third dimension; rather than just curving left or right, you may get an up and down wave in your herringbone stitch. The only way to know whether a particular combination of different sized beads will give you your desired result is to try!

If you add larger beads into the middle of the beadwork, or intermittently, you can get a different effect (figure 21).

Forcing beads out into the third dimension creates a shape that varies from the standard flat fabric of herringbone stitch. It adds exciting texture on the surface of the beadwork. You no longer have a flat surface; now you have a three-dimensional surface to work with (figure 22).

VARYING LADDER START AND FINISH

Lastly, playing with how and where the ladders start and end can yield fascinating results. Rather than starting each ladder off the same row, you can actually add new ladders that begin after several previously stitched rows, as in Fern Earrings. To begin a new ladder off an existing ladder, after you add a pair of beads onto the existing ladder, don't do the step up. Instead, pick up a new bead and ladder it to the bead your thread is exiting on the existing ladder (figure 23). Then ladder a second bead to the first (figure 24).

You'll notice that this brings your thread out on the bottom of the two beads added; if you continued without correcting this, you would be working in the opposite direction of the first ladder. To continue working in the same direction as the first ladder, stitch up through the first bead added (figure 25).

To modify the look slightly and create a pointy start to the new ladder, add a bottom bead beneath the two new beads (figure 26).

You can then work the new ladder from this new two-bead base.

Remember, any time you want to add a new ladder to your herringbone stitch, all you have to do is figure out a way to add two extra beads, and these will act as the first row of your new ladder.

two-ladder tennis bracelet

This simple bracelet introduces the technique of embellishing on top of flat herringbone stitch. The result is a simple, elegant bracelet that can be stitched in less than two hours and worn every day.

YOU'LL NEED

Size 8° metallic bronze iris cut seed beads, 9 g

Size 11° metallic bronze round seed beads, 1 g

Topaz AB crystal margarita bead, 8 mm

41 metallic purple crystal bicone beads, 4 mm

Size 12 beading needles

Polyethylene or other strong beading thread

Scissors

Work surface

TECHNIQUES

Flat Herringbone Stitch

Single-Ladder Herringbone Stitch

Ladder Stitch

DIMENSIONS

6 inches (15.2 cm) long

DIFFICULTY LEVEL

Easy beginner

OVERVIEW

Initially, you'll stitch the base of the bracelet in flat herringbone stitch. After that you'll make the closure with a button loop and a margarita bead, which acts as the button. Finally, you'll finish the bracelet by weaving from one end to the other adding embellishments.

BASE

1 To begin, needle up a wingspan of thread and ladder together two 8's.

2 Ladder a third 8°, then a fourth.

3 With your thread emerging from an end bead, start flat herringbone stitch. Envision the four beads you laddered together in steps 2 and 3 as two ladders, side by side. Pick up two 8°s, then stitch down through the next 8° in the laddered group and up through the next. Pick up two 8°s, then stitch down through the next 8° in the laddered group. Catch the thread that runs between the bottom pair of beads in the current ladder. Then stitch back up through the second bead in each pair in the ladder.

4 Continue adding rows of beads in this manner.

For a 6-inch (15.2 cm) bracelet, stitch 61 rows. For each additional inch (2.5 cm), stitch 10 additional rows.

BUTTON LOOP

5 After the last row, switch to single-ladder herringbone stitch on one of the ladders. Add five pairs of 8°s to one ladder.

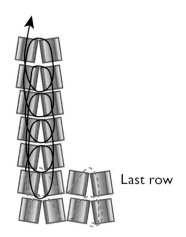

Last row

6 Go back through the second bead in the last pair. Add one 8° in ladder stitch; add another 8° in ladder stitch so you have four 8°s laddered together. Bring your thread out of the last bead so you are working toward the bracelet base.

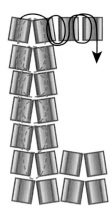

7 Using the two beads you just added in ladder stitch as the base, add four pairs of 8°s in single-ladder herringbone stitch. Connect the ladder to the bracelet base by picking up the open pair of 8°s in the last row of the bracelet. Weave through the beadwork and bring your thread out of one of the end beads on the button loop.

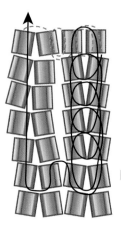

Last row

LAST ROW

8 Pick up three 8°s and stitch into the other end bead, then through the beadwork of the button loop. This step hides the bead holes on the visible end of the bracelet. Secure your thread in the beadwork and trim it.

BUTTON AND EMBELLISHMENTS

9 Start a new 1-yard (91.4 cm) thread at the beginning of the bracelet base. Referring to the figures below, bring your thread out of the second bead of the first ladder in the second row (red dot) and pick up two 11°s, the margarita bead, and one 11°. Stitch back through the margarita bead and the two 11°s, then through the second bead of the first ladder in the third row (blue dot). Stitch back through the first bead of the second ladder of the third row (green dot), then through the button beads, back down and into the first bead in the second ladder in the second row (black dot).

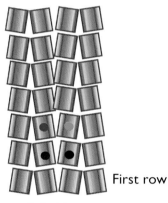

First row

Side View

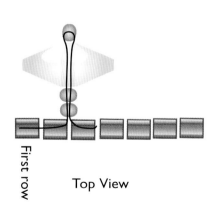

First row

Top View

Repeat the thread path at least one more time to reinforce, because there will be a lot of stress on this button when you close the bracelet.

10 Using the same thread, weave through the beadwork and bring your thread out of the second bead in the second ladder of the sixth row. Pick up one 11°, one bicone, and one 11°. Working in the same direction, stitch through the first bead in the first ladder in the seventh row and the first bead in the first ladder in the eighth row. This allows the embellishment to sit neatly across the bracelet base.

Pick up another set of embellishment beads, then stitch through the second bead in the second ladder in the next two rows. Continue this pattern along the entire length of the bracelet base, stopping just before the button loop. Then secure your thread in the beadwork and trim it.

variation

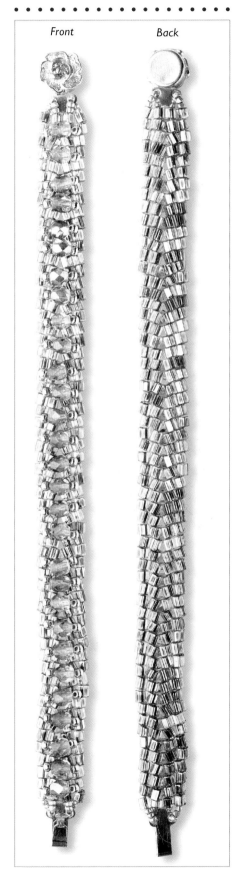

Front   Back

earth mother earrings

The look of these earrings can be drastically altered by changing the color and finish of the beads. The earthy tones in the beads I chose inspired their name.

YOU'LL NEED

Size 15° bronze-lined amber round seed beads, 1 g

Size 11° satin light lavender cylinder beads, 1 g

Size 10° matte metallic khaki iris cylinder beads, 2 g

Size 8° ceylon pale orchid round seed beads, 3 g

76 pale peach AB crystal bicones, 3 mm

76 matte metallic khaki iris cube beads, 4 mm

2 gold-plated ear wires

Size 12 and 13 beading needles*

Gray beading thread

Scissors

Work surface

* You'll bead this project with size 12 needles, but keep size 13s on hand in case the small holes in the bronze-lined 15° beads cause you trouble.

TECHNIQUES

Ladder Stitch

Flat Herringbone Stitch

DIMENSIONS

2³/₈ (6 cm) inches long

DIFFICULTY LEVEL

Easy Beginner

OVERVIEW

Although they may seem complicated at first, these earrings are merely made by stitching 38 rows of flat herringbone stitch three ladders wide. The only tricky part is seamlessly joining the first row and the last to give the appearance of a continuous ring.

START

1 Needle up a wingspan of thread. Ladder together the following beads to form your first row: one 15°, one 11°, one 10°, one 8°, one 3-mm bicone, and one 4-mm cube. Leave just enough of a tail to secure in the beadwork later and trim.

2 Stitch a second row in flat herringbone stitch, adding the same beads atop the beads in the first row. At the end of the row, catch a thread loop on the underside of row 1, then bring your thread out of the last bead added.

3 Stitch 36 more rows identical to the second row for a total of 38 rows. As you stitch, your beadwork should begin to curve dramatically.

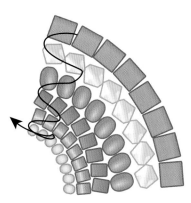

4 After adding the 38th row, stitch as though you're adding a 39th row using the beads in the first row. This creates a seamless join because the thread path between the first and last rows is identical to all the other rows.

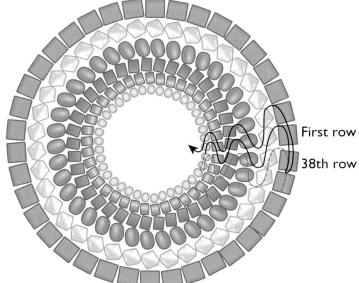

First row

38th row

5 After you go through the last pair of beads in the row, catch a loop of thread to turn around and retrace the thread path between the first and second row, then bring your thread out of the cube bead on the end. Pick up nine 15°s and the bottom loop of one ear wire, then go through the same cube bead again. Repeat the thread path through the 15°s and cube bead, then secure your thread in the beadwork and trim it.

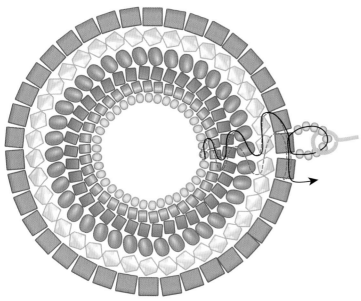

6 Secure the tail thread in the beadwork and trim it. Repeat all the steps to make a second earring.

lacy wrap choker

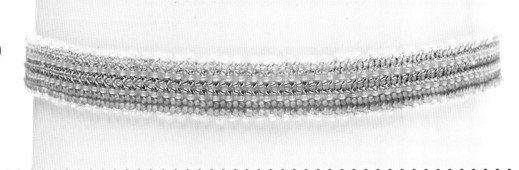

This choker is simple to stitch and makes a stylish addition to your wardrobe. The design is versatile, too. If you prefer, you can wear it wrapped twice around your wrist as a bracelet.

YOU'LL NEED

Size 15° round seed beads:

    A, matte translucent amethyst AB, 1 g

    B, copper-lined crystal, 1 g

    C, bronze-lined peridot AB, 1 g

    D, ceylon cream, 2 g

Antique brass filigree button, 24 mm

Size 12 beading needles

Rose beading thread

Scissors

Work surface

TECHNIQUES

Ladder Stitch

Flat Herringbone Stitch

Single-Ladder Herringbone Stitch

DIMENSIONS

12½ inches (31.8 cm) long

DIFFICULTY LEVEL

Experienced beginner

OVERVIEW
You'll start by laddering together the first row of beads, then use that row as a base to build the rest of the choker in flat herringbone stitch. Stitch each ladder with a different bead and add 15°s between ladders and on the herringbone edges for a lacy appearance. Finish the project with a button and loop closure.

BASE
Needle up a wingspan of thread. Leaving an 18-inch (35.7 cm) tail, ladder together the following beads to form your first row: A, A, B, B, C, and C.

Row 2: Add one row of 15°s in flat herringbone stitch. Match the 15° in each ladder to the beads in the base. At the end of the row, catch a thread on the underside of row 1 and bring your thread out of the last bead added to step up.

Row 3: Continuing in herringbone stitch, add two As to the first ladder, then add one D between the first and second ladder. Add two Bs to the middle ladder, then add one D between the second and third ladder. Add two Cs to the third ladder, then pick up one D and stitch back through the C before it and step up through the last C added.

Row 4: Continuing in herringbone stitch, add two Cs to the third ladder, then stitch through the D between ladders added in row 3. Add two Bs, then stitch through the D between ladders. Add two As, then pick up one D and stitch back through the A before it and step up through the last A added.

Rows 5 and on: Repeat the pattern established in rows 3 and 4 to stitch the remainder of the length of the choker. As you work, check the length against your neck to determine when to stop stitching—keep in mind that the closure will add about 1 inch (2.5 cm) to the overall length.

BUTTON LOOP

1 Finish the last row by adding two As to the first ladder in herringbone stitch, then stitch through one D between the first and second ladder, two Bs in the herringbone, and one D between the second and third ladder—you do *not* add a pair of Bs to the second ladder. Add two Cs to the third ladder, then pick up one D and stitch back through the C before it and step up through the last C added.

2 Switching to single-ladder herringbone stitch, add 20 pairs of Cs to the third ladder, reversing direction after each stitch by adding a pair of Ds to each edge. After adding the 20th pair, your thread will end up on the inside of the ladder.

3 Ladder one pair of Bs to the first bead in the last two rows of the third ladder.

4 Add one pair of Bs to the first pair of Bs.

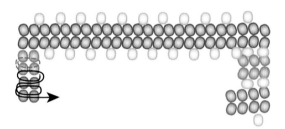

5 Ladder one pair of As to the second pair of Bs; ladder one pair of As to the first pair of As. Then weave your thread into the beadwork and trim it.

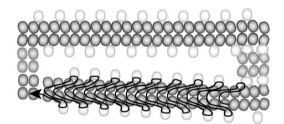

6 Needle up 1 yard (91.4 cm) of thread and weave in at the end of the A ladder and bring it out of the last row of As. Switch to single-ladder herringbone stitch and add 20 pairs of As, with Ds on the ends of the ladder as in step 2.

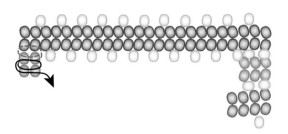

7 To join the single ladder of As to the two laddered pairs of As at the end of the button loop, stitch as though you're picking up the first pair of beads in herringbone stitch and add one D on the outside of the ladder, then step up. Pick up the second pair of beads in the laddered pairs, add one D on the outside of the ladder, then step up. Weave your thread into the beadwork and trim it.

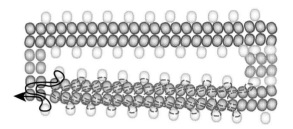

8 Needle up the tail thread. Weave up through the first bead in the first ladder in the second, third, fourth, and fifth rows. Stitch back through the second bead in the first ladder's fifth row, the D between ladders, and the first bead in the second ladder's fifth row.

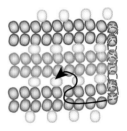

9 Pick up five Bs and the button shank, then stitch into the second bead in the second ladder's fifth row. Repeat the thread path as many times as the bead holes will allow to reinforce. Then secure your thread in the beadwork and trim it.

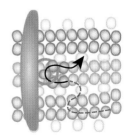

poseidon's gem bracelet

Flat herringbone stitch is all you need to create this elegant bracelet. By using different sized beads, you can make the bracelet weave in a pleasing, sinusoidal pattern.

YOU'LL NEED

Size 15° matte metallic eggplant iris round seed beads, 1 g

Size 11° gold luster taupe cylinder beads, 1 g

Size 11° sand-lined crystal round seed beads, 1 g

Size 8° matte metallic bronze round seed beads, 3 g

Size 6° metallic dark bronze round seed beads, 9 g

72 peridot luster fire-polished rounds, 4 mm

Bronze freshwater pearl, 10 mm

Size 12 beading needles

White beading thread

Scissors

Work surface

TECHNIQUES

Ladder Stitch

Flat Herringbone Stitch

DIMENSIONS

6 inches (15.2 cm) long

DIFFICULTY LEVEL

Experienced beginner

OVERVIEW

You'll create three ladders of flat herringbone stitch, using a different bead for each half of each ladder. Next, you'll stitch with the same beads on each ladder half for nine rows, then reverse the order of the beads. The waving shape is a result of the differences in bead sizes.

START

Needle up a wingspan of thread. Leaving a tail 18 inches (45.7 cm) long, ladder together the following beads in order: one 15°, one 11° cylinder bead, one 11° round, one 8°, one 6°, and one fire-polished round. This counts as row 1.

ROWS 2–9

Stitch one row of beads in herringbone stitch, picking up the same beads as in the first row, so each bead sits atop a like bead. After adding the last pair of beads, catch a loop of thread on the underside of row 1 and bring your thread out of the last bead added.

Stitch row 3 in the same fashion, but this time add the beads in reverse order.

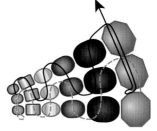

Repeat row 2 and row 3 three more times for a total of nine rows. Your beadwork will curve dramatically.

After the ninth row, add the beads in the same order as in row 3 so that different beads sit atop the beads in row 9.

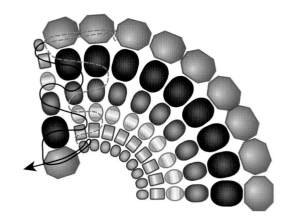

Stitch eight more rows, adding the same beads atop the previous row of beads for a total of nine rows in the section. The beadwork will curve in the direction opposite the first section. The two sections curving in opposite directions constitute one complete repeat.

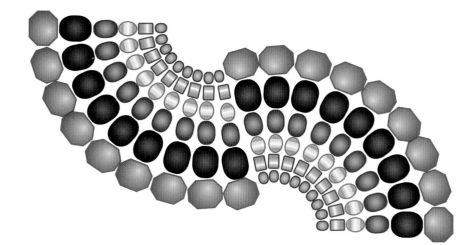

FINISH

Each complete repeat creates about 1½ inches (3.8 cm) of beadwork. The closure will add a miniscule amount to the finished length. Bead the bracelet to the desired length, then weave through the last row and bring your thread out between the 11°s in the last row and the second-to-last row.

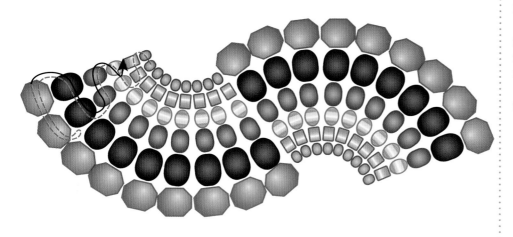

Pick up twenty-six 15°s. Stitch into the 6° in the second-to-last row. Weave through the beadwork and bring your thread out between the 11°s in the last row and the second-to-last row. Reinforce the beadwork by repeating the thread path through the loop of 15°s as many times as the bead holes will allow.

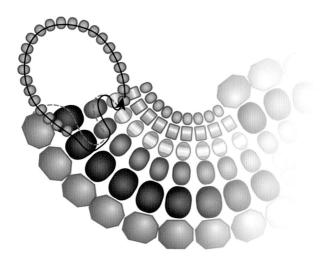

Weave your thread into the beadwork, secure it, and trim it.

Needle up your tail thread. Weave through the beadwork and bring your thread out between the 8°s in the second and third rows. Pick up two 15°s, the freshwater pearl, and one 15°. Skip the last 15° and stitch back through the pearl and two 15°s last added, then stitch through the 6° in the third row. Stitch out through the 8° in the third row and repeat the thread path through the 15°s and pearl at least one more time to reinforce.

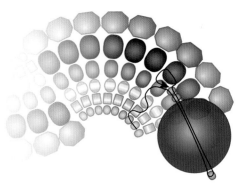

Weave the thread into the beadwork, secure it, and trim it. To close your bracelet, push the pearl through the loop of 15°s.

starry night necklace

Because the silver rondelles and bicones embellishing the base beadwork twinkle like stars, this necklace is named after Van Gogh's famous painting.

Size 11° navy-lined crystal round seed beads, 8 g

3.4-mm palladium magatama drop beads, 4 g

9 silver crystal rondelles, 6 x 8 mm

Size 15° palladium round seed beads, < 1 g

21 silver crystal bicone beads, 3 mm

Crystal butterfly pendant, 12 x 28 mm

Size 12 beading needles

Dark-colored beading thread

Thread bobbin

Scissors

Work surface

• • • • • • • • • • • • • • • •

TECHNIQUES

Ladder Stitch

Flat Herringbone Stitch

Single-Ladder Herringbone Stitch

Embellishment

• • • • • • • • • • • • • • • •

DIMENSIONS

14 inches (35.6 cm) long

• • • • • • • • • • • • • • • •

DIFFICULTY LEVEL

Intermediate

To successfully make this project, be sure to purchase Miyuki's or Toho's magatamas. The shape of other drop beads is different—they're too wide in the direction of the hole—so the project won't work up as nicely if you use those.

OVERVIEW

First, you'll create a laddered base the entire length of the necklace. You'll then weave back and forth along the base, adding beads in flat herringbone stitch, then switch to a single-ladder herringbone to incorporate some embellishments. Finally, you'll add a second layer of embellishments in the center region of the necklace and add the crystal butterfly and loop closure to the ends of the necklace.

BASE

Determine the desired length of your finished necklace, keeping in mind the closure will add about 1 inch (2.5 cm) to the finished length. To begin, needle up a wingspan of thread and ladder together two 11°s. Continue adding 11°s in ladder stitch to create a single row that spans the entire length of the necklace. This counts as row 1.

Make sure you have an even number of beads laddered together in this initial row and an odd number of pairs so there's a single pair at the center. For example, a necklace 14 inches (35.6 cm) long would have 162 beads laddered together and 81 pairs of beads.

Row 2: When you've added the last 11°, reverse direction and add pairs of 11°s to each laddered pair in flat herringbone stitch, along the entire length of the necklace. At the end of the row, catch a thread on the underside of row 1 and bring your thread out of the last bead added to step up.

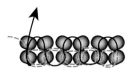

Row 3: When you add the final pair of 11°s, catch the thread bridge between the first pair of laddered beads, and go back through the last bead added. Add another row of 11°s in flat herringbone from one end of the necklace to the other.

Locate the center pair of 11°s on the original laddered base. You'll need to constantly reference this center ladder, so stick a needle or pin into each bead in the pair to mark them. Weave in your current working thread and trim it. Needle up two wingspans of thread. Weave the thread into one 11° in the center pair, then bring your thread out of the working end of the ladder.

Needle up the other end of the thread, weave it through the 11° adjacent to the center ladder, then bring it out of the working end of that ladder. Center your thread so each end is equal in length.

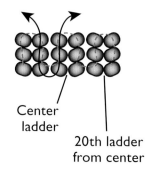

Center ladder

20th ladder from center

Row 4: You'll now work one half of the necklace, plus the center, with the first half of the thread, and the other half of the necklace with the second half of the thread. When not in use, weave one thread around an old thread bobbin to keep it out of the way. With the first thread, do 21 stitches of flat herringbone with 11°s from the center out. Note that this number *includes* the center ladder.

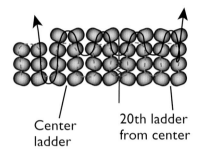

Center ladder   20th ladder from center

Row 5, first thread: Reverse direction; add one drop bead to the 20th and 19th ladders from the center in herringbone, then add 11°s in herringbone stitch for 19 ladders (including center). **Second thread:** Reverse direction; add one drop bead to the end of the 20th and 19th ladders from the center in herringbone, then add 11°s in herringbone for 18 ladders.

20th ladder from center   Center ladder

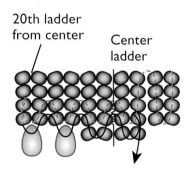

HANGING EMBELLISHMENTS

Now take up each ladder individually; add rows of beads in herringbone stitch as if you're working only one ladder at a time.

Starting with the center ladder, add 15 rows of 11°s, then pick up fifteen 11°s, one rondelle, and fifteen 11°s. Stitch up through the column of 11°s that comprises the second bead of each pair you just added, then up two more 11°s. Stitch down through the bottom two 11°s in the first ladder from center. Add two rows of 11°s, then pick up two 11°s, one drop bead, and two 11°s. Stitch up through the column of 11°s that comprises the second bead of each pair you just added, then up two more 11°s.

Continue in this manner to reduce the number of beads in each column according to the figure below until you reach the 19th ladder from the center, alternating between ladders with a rondelle at the bottom and ladders with a drop bead at the bottom.

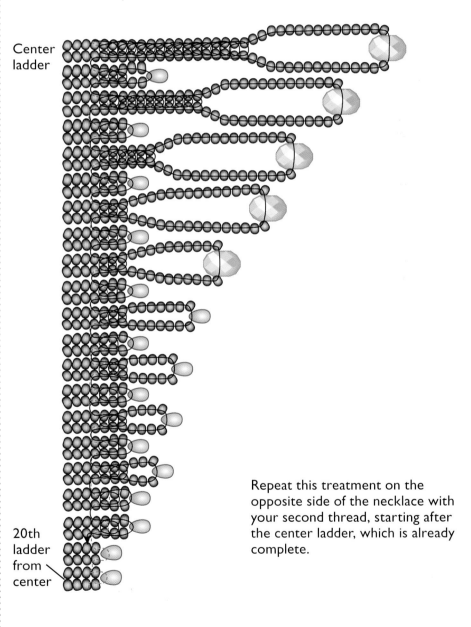

Center ladder

20th ladder from center

Repeat this treatment on the opposite side of the necklace with your second thread, starting after the center ladder, which is already complete.

SURFACE EMBELLISHMENTS

Pick up your first thread. Weave through the 20th ladder from the center to the 21st ladder from the center and bring your thread out of the first 11° in the bottom pair of 11°s. Pick up two 15°s, one bicone, and two 15°s. Stitch up through the second bead of the second pair of 11°s from bottom in the 19th ladder from the center. Stitch down through the first bead of this pair.

Repeat this embellishment in the same fashion, bridging between every other ladder, until you reach the center of the necklace; add the center embellishment. The embellishments are positioned over the longer ladders.

Weave your first thread into the beadwork, secure it, and trim it. Pick up your second thread. Repeat the surface embellishments on the other side of the necklace. Weave your second thread into the beadwork, secure it, and trim it.

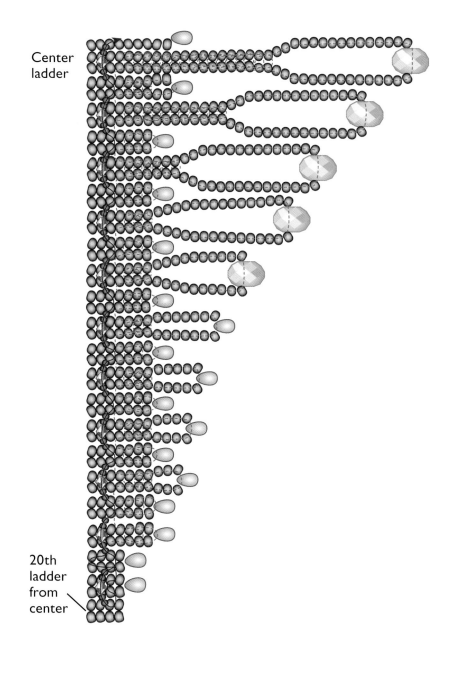

Center ladder

20th ladder from center

BOTTOMS OF REMAINING LADDERS, CLOSURE

Start a new thread in the 20th ladder from the center on one side of the necklace, then bring it out of the first bead of the bottom pair in the 21st ladder from the center, oriented so you are working from the center of the necklace out to the end. Add one drop bead to the bottom of each ladder, including the last ladder.

Bring your thread out of the last ladder, between the first and second pair of beads. Pick up seven 11°s, one drop bead, the butterfly crystal, and three drop beads. Stitch back through the crystal, drop bead, and seven 11°s, and into the last ladder. Repeat the thread path several times to strengthen the connection. Then secure your thread in the beadwork and trim it.

Start a new thread in the 20th ladder from center on the other side of the necklace. Add drop beads to the bottom of each ladder as you did on the first side, then bring your thread out of the last ladder between the first and second bead pair. Pick up twenty-six 11°s; these will be the loop around the butterfly crystal, so check to make sure that's enough to fit around it. Adjust as necessary, then stitch back into the last ladder.

Repeat the thread path several times to strengthen the connection, then secure your thread in the beadwork and trim it.

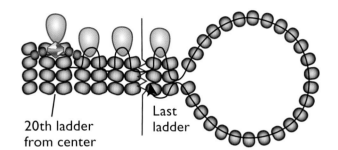

20th ladder
from center

Last
ladder

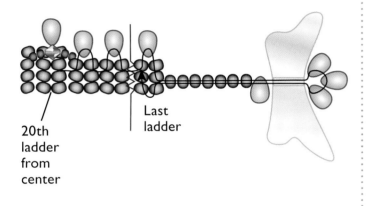

20th
ladder
from
center

Last
ladder

fern earrings

This project manipulates single-ladder herringbone stitch to construct miniature lifelike ferns with a texture that mimics the appearance of living plants. Decorate your ears with these funky pieces of foliage!

YOU'LL NEED

Size 11° round seed beads:

    A, metallic olive gold iris, 2 g

    B, metallic dark copper iris, 2 g

Size 15° metallic bronze iris round seed beads, 1 g

Size 8° silk dark bronze iris round seed beads, 1 g

10 magenta freshwater potato pearls, 4 to 5 mm

10 silver champagne AB crystal rondelles, 5 x 3 mm

2 gold-plated ear wires

Size 12 beading needles

Olive beading thread

Scissors

Work surface

TECHNIQUES

Ladder Stitch

Single-Ladder Herringbone Stitch

Fringing

DIMENSIONS

2½ (6.4 cm) inches

DIFFICULTY LEVEL

Advanced

OVERVIEW

You'll create one half of the fern by stitching single ladders of herringbone stitch—the *pinnae,* as the little leaflets on a fern are called—then start each new ladder from the previous one, using ladder stitch. Then you'll create the second half of the fern and zip—a beading term that means "connect"—the two halves together using 8°s. Lastly, you'll add fringe at the base of the fern and the ear wire. Throughout this project the term *pinnae* is used—it's plural for *pinna.*

SIDE 1

Each pinna is offset from the previous one, so they don't line up exactly. This creates a natural, tapered shape.

> Beads may be added to or subtracted from each row to make thinner or thicker ferns.

Side 1 Pinnae

Pinna #	1st bead added	2nd/3rd bead added	Subsequent bead pairs								Top bead
1	A	A/A	A/A	A/A	A/B	B/B	B/B	B/B	B/B	15°/15°	B
2	A	A/A	A/B	A/B	A/B	B/B	B/B	B/B	15°/15°		B
3	A	A/A	A/B	B/B	B/B	B/B	B/B	15°/15°			B
4	A	A/A	A/B	B/B	B/B	B/B	15°/15°				B
5	A	A/A	A/B	B/B	B/B	15°/15°					B
6	A	A/A	A/A	B/B	15°/15°						B
7	A	A/B	A/B	15°/15°							B
8	A	A/B	15°/15°								B
9	A	A/B									B

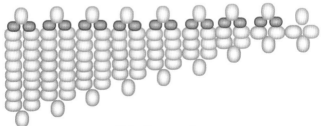

Side 1 overview

1 Needle up a wingspan of thread. Anchor one A and leave just enough of a tail to weave into the beadwork later and trim. This is your *bottom bead*.

2 Pick up your first pair of beads, labeled *2nd/3rd bead added* in the figure below. Stitch through the bottom bead again, then through the first bead just added.

2nd bead added   3rd bead added

3 Pick up your second pair of beads and ladder it to the pair below in single-ladder herringbone stitch.

4 Add the third pair of beads the same way.

5 Add the remaining bead pairs indicated using single-ladder herringbone stitch.

6 Add the top bead to the end of the ladder, then stitch down through the column comprised of the second bead in each pair, bringing your thread out of a bead in the second pair. You've finished the first pinna.

Top bead

7 To start the next pinna, ladder the first bead in the first pair to the bead from which your thread is emerging.

1st bead added

Note: The first three beads added in pinna 1 differ from the first three beads added in all of the subsequent pinnae.

8 Pick up the second bead plus the third bead, then stitch through the first bead again.

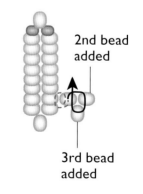

2nd bead added

3rd bead added

9 Add the second pair in single-ladder herringbone stitch. Then ladder the first bead of the second pair to the adjacent bead on the previous pinna. This holds the pinnae together. Do this laddering stitch with the first half of all the pairs in the pinna.

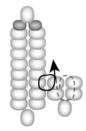

10 Continue stitching the pinnae in the same fashion, following the chart. Because there's only one pair of beads in the ninth pinna, you cannot offset it from the eighth pinna.

Pinna 8

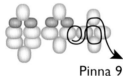

Pinna 9

11 To finish side 1, stitch a pair of Bs to the second bead in the only pair in the ninth pinna. Use this pair as a base to stitch the following pairs of beads in single-ladder herringbone stitch: one pair of Bs and four pairs of 15°s/Bs. At the end, add three 15°s and three Bs, then stitch down through the column of 11°s, the second bead in the bead pair of the ninth pinna, and the bottom bead of the ninth pinna. Leave this thread hanging for the attachment of side 2 later.

SIDE 2

Needle up 1 yard (91.4 cm) of thread. Start side 2 exactly as you started side 1, referring to the figure below for the specific beads in each pinna.

Pinna #	1st bead added	2nd/3rd bead added	Subsequent bead pairs			Top bead
Side 2 Pinnae						
1	A	A/B	A/B	B/B	15°/15°	B
2	A	A/B	B/B	15°/15°		B
3	A	A/B	B/B	15°/15°		B
4	A	A/B	15°/15°			B
5	A	A/B				B
6	A	A/B				B

Side 2 is purposefully shorter and stouter than side 1. When you complete side 2, secure your thread in the beadwork and trim it.

Side 2 overview

ASSEMBLE

• Align the two sides of the fern so the longest pinnae are at the bottom and the shortest pinnae are at the top. The bottom beads of each side should both be on the inside. Needle up the hanging thread from side 1. This thread should be emerging from the ninth pinna's bottom bead. Stitch through the bottom bead of the sixth pinna on side 2, then through the bottom bead of the eighth pinna on side 1. Pick up one 8°. Stitch through the bottom bead of the seventh pinna on side 1, the bottom bead of the fifth pinna on side 2, and the bottom bead of the sixth pinna on side 1.

• Pick up one 8°. Stitch through the bottom bead of the fifth pinna on side 1, the bottom bead of the fourth pinna on side 2, and the bottom bead of the fourth pinna on side 1.

• Pick up one 8°. Stitch through the bottom bead of the third pinna on side 1, then the bottom bead of the third pinna on side 2.

• Pick up one 8°. Stitch through the bottom bead of the second pinna on side 1, then the bottom bead of the second pinna on side 2. Pick up one 8°. Stitch through the bottom bead of the first pinna on side 1, then the bottom bead of the first pinna on side 2.

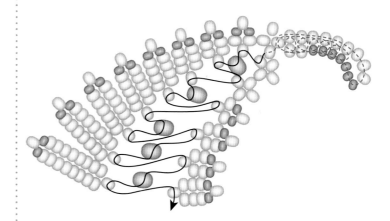

FRINGE AND EAR WIRE

• Pick up six As, seven 15°s, and the ear wire. Stitch back through the last A. Pick up one 15°, one pearl, and one 15°. Stitch back through the pearl and 15° and through the next A.

• Pick up one 15°, one pearl, and one 15°. Stitch back through the pearl and 15° and through the next A.

• Pick up two 15°s, one rondelle, and one 15°. Stitch back through the rondelle and two 15°s, then through the next A. Pick up two 15°s, one rondelle, and one 15°. Stitch back through the rondelle and two 15°s, then through the next A.

• Pick up four 15°s, one pearl, and one 15°. Stitch back through the pearl and four 15°s, then through the next A. Pick up four 15°s, one rondelle, and one 15°. Stitch back through the rondelle and four 15°s, then through the bottom bead of the first pinna on side 1.

• Reverse direction in the beadwork and stitch back through the bottom bead of the first pinna on side 1, then the first A. Pick up four 15°s, one pearl, and one 15°. Stitch back through the pearl and four 15°s, then through the next A.

• Pick up four 15°s, one rondelle, and one 15°. Stitch back through the rondelle and four 15°s, then through the next A. Pick up one 15°, one pearl, and one 15°. Stitch back through the pearl and 15° and through the next A.

• Pick up two 15°s, one rondelle, and one 15°. Stitch back through the rondelle and two 15°s, then through the next two As and the loop of 15°s that holds the ear wire. Stitch down the line of As and secure your thread in the beadwork, then trim it.

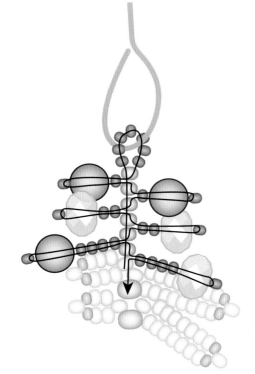

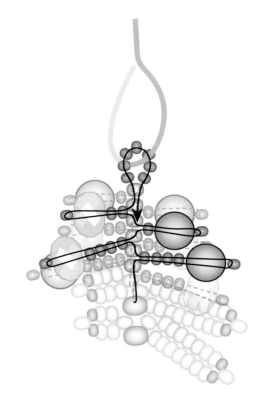

Repeat all the steps to make a second earring.

4

tubular herringbone stitch

Tubular herringbone stitch is incredibly versatile and interesting. It makes a wonderful, flexible rope in two-ladder, three-ladder, or even four-ladder form. Create tubes from a single type of bead, or use different beads to create interesting details, like in Sweet Sets Necklace.

My favorite type of herringbone tube is the two-ladder form, which is showcased in many of the projects in this chapter. Far from being mundane, this stitch is incredibly versatile when you use a little imagination in choosing beads and creating embellishments. In addition to the beauty and versatility of tubular herringbone stitch, it works up quickly compared to other tubular beading stitches because you add two beads with each stitch.

START

There are two basic techniques for beginning tubular herringbone stitch: the laddering method and the Ndebele method.

Laddering Method

This technique consists of laddering together the beads needed for the first row of tubular herringbone stitch. As for flat herringbone stitch, the number of beads you'll need in the first row is twice the number of ladders

FIGURE I

in the project. The major difference between this technique, when it's used to begin tubular herringbone stitch, and the flat version is the first bead and the last bead need to be laddered together at the end, so you have a tube (figure 1). For a closer look at creating a ladder, check out Ladder Stitch in chapter 2 (page 13).

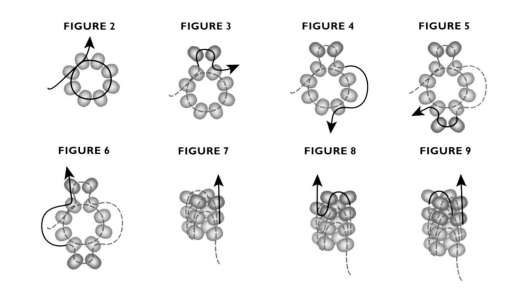

FIGURE 2 FIGURE 3 FIGURE 4 FIGURE 5

FIGURE 6 FIGURE 7 FIGURE 8 FIGURE 9

Ndebele Method

This method initially looks much more complicated than the laddering method, but it has advantages. It produces the first three rows of your herringbone tube, as opposed to the laddering method, which creates only the first row. More important, this method creates a base that has the same thread pattern as the rest of the herringbone tube.

This allows you to do two things. You have the option of working from the tail side of the tube and adding rows in the opposite direction, with no interruption in the pattern or look of the beadwork. In addition, you can pull out the first few rows of beads if the base doesn't come out perfectly, because the thread remains loose enough to do this.

Always begin by picking up the number of beads that equals four times the number of ladders in your tube. For our example, we'll start two-ladder tubular herringbone stitch. Needle up 1 yard (91.4 cm) of thread and pick up eight beads. Holding the thread tail, slide the beads down toward the tail, leaving just enough thread to secure in the beadwork later.

Stitch through the first two beads again to form a ring (figure 2).

Grasp the tail tightly in your nondominant hand while working. Pick up two beads and stitch through the next bead in the ring. If you use contrasting color beads here, you'll be better able to distinguish your two ladders later (figure 3).

Skip over the next two beads in the ring and stitch through the third (figure 4).

Pick up two beads (contrasting colors if desired) and stitch through the next bead in the ring (figure 5).

Skip over the next two beads in the ring and stitch through the third, then step up through the next bead (figure 6).

If you pull the tail thread and working thread in opposite directions, you should begin to see the two ladders. The contrasting color beads you added are the pairs of beads at the tops of your two ladders (figure 7).

CONTINUE THE TUBE

Now that you have the initial base, work in herringbone from one ladder to the other and then back. Pick up a pair of beads, then stitch down through the adjacent bead in the same ladder. Stitch up through the top bead in the next ladder (figure 8).

Pick up a pair of beads, then stitch down through the adjacent bead in the same ladder. Stitch up through the top *two* beads in the next ladder (figure 9). Stitching through the top two beads, rather than one, prepares you for the next row. This is called the "step up." (When stitching non-twisted tubular herringbone, always step up at the end of the row. We'll cover twisted tubular herringbone stitch in the next chapter.)

You now have four rows of two-ladder tubular herringbone stitch. Work the rest of the tube exactly like row 4, which is the last row you stitched.

spindle earrings

These simple earrings show how you can use different sized beads in herringbone stitch to create shape and volume. You can create totally different looks by using the same basic pattern and experimenting with the type, shape, and finish of the beads used, plus adding different drops onto the bottoms of the earrings!

YOU'LL NEED

Size 15° metallic dark copper seed beads, 1 g

Size 11° silk dark copper iris seed beads, 1 g

Size 8° dyed rose bronze silver-lined alabaster seed beads, 1 g

3-mm copper iris cube beads, 1 g

2 gold-plated ear wires

Size 12 beading needles

Beading thread

Scissors

Work surface

TECHNIQUES

Ladder Stitch

Two-Ladder Tubular Herringbone Stitch

DIMENSIONS

1¼ inches (3.2 cm) long

DIFFICULTY LEVEL

Easy beginner

OVERVIEW

You'll start by laddering together the first two rows of beads, and then build your two-ladder tubular herringbone stitch off of this base. You'll add a small embellishment onto the bottom of the earrings and an ear wire at the top.

BASE

1 Needle up a wingspan of thread. Pick up four 15°s and stitch through the first four beads again to ladder the pairs of beads together, leaving just enough of a tail to secure in the beadwork later, and trim.

2 Ladder two more pairs of 15°s.

3 Ladder the last pair of 15°s to the first pair.

MAIN EARRING TUBE

4 Continuing in tubular herringbone, add beads to successive rows.

Row 3: Pick up two 11°s, then stitch down through the next bead in row 2, and up through the top bead on the next ladder. Pick up two 11°s, then stitch down through the next bead in row 2 and up through the top two beads in the first ladder to step up for the next row.

Row 4: Add 8°s.
Row 5: Add 3-mm cubes.
Row 6: Add 8°s.
Row 7: Add 11°s.
Row 8: Add 15°s.

FINISH

5 Pick up one 8° and one 15°. Stitch back through the 8° and the other side of the ladder, through the whole tube and out of row 1.

6 Pick up five 15°s and the ear wire loop. Stitch into the other side of row 1 and through the whole tube, out the end of row 8.

7 Repeat the thread path through the 8° and 15°, then stitch through the other ladder and the ear wire loop, then back through the other side of the ladder and out row 8. Secure both threads in the beadwork and trim them.

8 Repeat all steps to make a second earring.

component bracelet

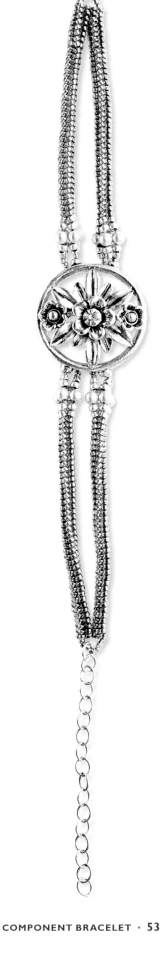

This bracelet provides a great way to incorporate a metal spacer or other component as a focal piece. As long as the component has four holes, it may be included in this project.

YOU'LL NEED

Size 15° silver-lined black diamond AB seed beads, 4 g

Size 11° silver-plated cylinder beads, 1 g

Size 11° permanent finish galvanized lime round seed beads, 1 g

16 baby blue glass pearls, 3 mm

Two-strand circular focal component, 1 inch (2.5 cm) in diameter

Silver-plated lobster clasp

2¼ inch (5.7 cm) silver-plated soldered chain, 3 x 4 mm

Size 12 beading needles

Polyethylene or other strong beading thread

Scissors

Work surface

TECHNIQUES

Two-Ladder Tubular Herringbone Stitch

DIMENSIONS

6 inches (15.2 cm), not including clasp or chain

DIFFICULTY LEVEL

Easy beginner

OVERVIEW

You'll stitch each of the four herringbone tubes separately, and join their ends to the focal component. You'll then join the pairs of herringbone tubes and attach the lobster clasp and chain.

TUBES

Needle up a wingspan of thread. Start a two-ladder herringbone tube with all 15°s using either start method. Leave a tail 12 inches (30.5 cm) long. Stitch 40 rows total with 15°s. Stitch row 41 with all 11° cylinders, row 42 with 11° rounds, row 43 with pearls, row 44 with 11° rounds, and row 45 with 11° cylinders.

ATTACH FOCAL COMPONENT

Pick up one 15°, then stitch through one of the four holes in the focal component from outside to inside; pick up five 15°s, then stitch into a cylinder bead in row 45.

Stitch out of the adjacent cylinder bead in row 45, then through the six 15°s and focal component hole, and into the fourth bead in row 45. Repeat the thread path several more times to reinforce the connection, then secure your thread in the beadwork, and trim it.

Repeat three more times to create and attach three more tubes to the focal component.

CLOSURE

Needle up the tail thread on one of your herringbone tubes. Line up the end of the tube with the end of the adjacent tube. Ladder the adjacent beads in rows 1 and 2 of one tube to the beads in rows 1 and 2 of the other tube.

Ladder together the adjacent beads in rows 1 and 2 of ladder 2 of each herringbone tube.

Weave through the end of the tube, bringing your thread out of a bead in row 1 on the tube end. Pick up three 15°s, the lobster claw, and three 15°s. Stitch into the end bead in row 1 on the other tube.

Reverse direction, bringing your thread out of an adjacent bead in row 1, and repeat the thread path through the six 15°s and lobster claw ring, then into the end of the other tube. Repeat the thread path several times to reinforce the connection, then secure your thread in the beadwork and trim it. Secure the other hanging tail thread as well and trim it.

Repeat the previous steps on the other end of the bracelet, attaching the silver chain instead of the lobster clasp ring.

sweet sets necklace

Dress up tubular herringbone stitch by adding clusters of larger beads and glass pearls. This simple, charming necklace can by worn by itself, in multiples, or as a wrap bracelet.

YOU'LL NEED

Size 15° sparkling seafoam-lined crystal seed beads, 7 g

Size 11° satin seafoam cylinder beads, < 1 g

Size 11° stable galvanized gold seed beads, < 1 g

52 ecru glass pearls, 3 mm

Gold clasp

Size 12 beading needles

Polyethylene or other strong beading thread

Scissors

Work surface

TECHNIQUES

Ndebele Start

Two-Ladder Tubular Herringbone Stitch

DIMENSIONS

20½ inches (52.1 cm) long

DIFFICULTY LEVEL

Easy beginner

OVERVIEW

You'll start with the standard tubular herringbone base, then work a single two-ladder tube, size the necklace, and add the clasp.

BASE

Needle up a wingspan of thread and start a two-ladder tube of herringbone stitch with the Ndebele start method (page 50) using 15°s; leave an 18-inch (45.7 cm) tail.

Rows 4–32: Add 15°s.
Row 33: Add 11° cylinder beads.
Row 34: Add 11° seed beads.
Row 35: Add 3-mm pearls.
Row 36: Add 11° seed beads.
Row 37: Add 11° cylinder beads.

• Rows 33 through 37 constitute a pattern you'll repeat at different intervals between rows of 15°s.

• Stitch 32 rows with 15°s; do one pattern repeat.

• Stitch 32 rows with 15°s; do one pattern repeat.

• Stitch 24 rows with 15°s; one pattern repeat; 16 rows with 15°s; one pattern repeat; six rows with 15°s; one pattern repeat; six rows with 15°s; one pattern repeat; 16 rows with 15°s; one pattern repeat; 24 rows with 15°s; one pattern repeat; 32 rows with 15°s; one pattern repeat; 32 rows with 15°s; one pattern repeat; 32 rows with 15°s; one pattern repeat.

Needle up the tail thread and add one pattern repeat at the beginning of the necklace.

SIZING
The size of the necklace with no additional rows added will be about 20½ inches (52.1 cm). To add length, add rows of 15°s on each end of the necklace until your necklace is ½ inch (1.3 cm) short of the total desired length. Then add one pattern repeat on each end of the necklace.

CLOSURE
Bringing your thread out of the first bead in the first ladder of the end row, pick up four 15°s and one end of the clasp, then stitch down through the second bead in the first ladder and up through the first bead in the second ladder.

Pick up one 15° and stitch through the middle two 15°s in the group of four you just added. Pick up one 15° and stitch down through the second bead in the first ladder.

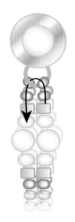

Repeat the thread path through all of the beads just added at least once more, then secure your thread in the beadwork, and trim it.

Repeat the process above to add the second half of the clasp to the other end of the necklace.

braided bracelet

This bracelet is a simple introduction to tubular herringbone that will give you a timeless piece of jewelry in a beautiful mixed-metal palette.

YOU'LL NEED

Size 11° round seed beads:

 A, silk copper, 6 g

 B, 24-karat gold-plated, 6 g

 C, stable galvanized silver, 6 g

Three-strand gold-plated slide clasp

Size 12 beading needles

Gray, yellow, and pink beading threads

Scissors

Work surface

TECHNIQUES

Ladder Stitch

Two-Ladder Tubular Herringbone
 Stitch

DIMENSIONS

8 inches (20.3 cm) long

DIFFICULTY LEVEL

Experienced beginner

OVERVIEW

You'll create three tubes, each with a different color bead, then weave the tubes together into a braid and secure each end to the clasp.

START

1 Needle up a wingspan of thread. Start a two-ladder herringbone tube with As using either method described in chapter 2. Start two identical tubes using B and C. Leave just enough of a tail thread to weave into the beadwork later on two of the tubes, and leave an 18-inch (45.7 cm) tail on the third tube.

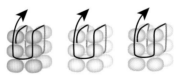

Use the gray thread when you work with the silver beads, yellow thread with the gold beads, and pink thread for the silk copper beads.

2 Stitch each tube using only the one bead color per tube to the desired length. Sixteen rows will give you about 1 inch (2.5 cm) of length in the finished, braided bracelet, and the clasp will add about ½ inch (1.3 cm) to the overall length.

BRAIDING AND CLOSURE

3 When each tube is the desired length, weave the thread from two of the three tubes into the beadwork, secure, and trim them. Place the ends of the three tubes next to each other. Using the remaining thread from the third tube, ladder together the end two rows of each tube on one side.

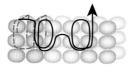

4 Weave to the other side, and ladder together the two end rows of each tube. Bring your thread out of the end bead on one side of the end tube.

5 Pick up two 11°s that match the tube your thread is emerging from, then stitch through one end loop of one half of the clasp and pick up two more of the same 11°s. Stitch through the first bead in the end row of the opposite ladder, then out through the first bead in the next row.

Reverse direction and stitch through the second bead in the second to last row and the second bead in the last row. Stitch back through the two 11°s last added, the clasp loop, and the two 11°s added at the beginning of this step, then into the second bead in the first ladder and the second bead in the next row. Weave through the beadwork and bring your thread out of the first bead in the first ladder of the middle tube.

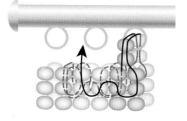

6 Repeat to attach the second and third clasp loops. Weave your thread into the beadwork, secure it, and trim it.

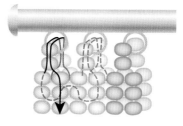

7 Weave the short tail threads of the first and second tubes into the beadwork, secure, and trim.

8 Braid the three tubes.

9 Needle up the long hanging tail thread. Stitch together the ends of the three tubes as you did on the first side of the bracelet in steps 3 and 4, then attach the other half of the slide clasp as in steps 5 and 6, being sure to orient it correctly.

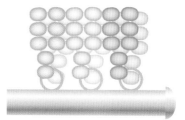

5
variations of tubular herringbone stitch

In this chapter, tubular herringbone becomes a whole new animal. Use it to create structural rhythmic curves like those in Victorian Elegance Necklace. Encapsulate negative space in projects such as Beaded Capsule Pendant. Stretch it to the limits with extreme variations like the supple chain in Willow Lariat. Get ready to take herringbone stitch to new heights!

ADDING BEADS BETWEEN LADDERS

Adding beads between ladders in tubular herringbone stitch basically forces the ladders apart, just like adding beads between flat herringbone stitch ladders. (The Pod Earrings show off this technique with beguiling results.) Due to the basic geometry of the stitch, when you add beads in this way, it increases the diameter of the tube (figure 1).

You can add different numbers and sizes of beads between ladders to get different effects, just as with adding beads between ladders in flat herringbone stitch.

FIGURE 1

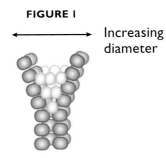

Increasing diameter

EMBELLISHMENT

Detailed here are ways to embellish a tube end as seen in Trumpet Lily Earrings and embellishing the length with variations of fringe. For even more possibilities, apply embellishment techniques from chapter 3 to your tubular herringbone creations.

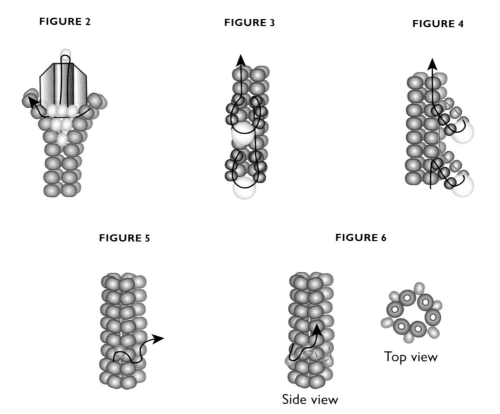

FIGURE 2   FIGURE 3   FIGURE 4

FIGURE 5   FIGURE 6

Side view   Top view

Increasing the size of the tube by adding beads between ladders offers the unique possibility of nestling larger beads into the ends of tubes. This makes for an attractive detail to a tapered tube end (figure 2).

You can also add groups, or loops, of beads off of ladders and between ladders, along the length of a tube. To add embellishments along a ladder, bring your thread out of it. Pick up the group of embellishment beads, then stitch through the other side of the ladder, working your way down the ladder. Stitch through one or more beads on the same side of the ladder, then pick up another group of embellishment beads and stitch through the opposite side of the ladder (figure 3).

Adding beads between ladders along the length of a tube is very similar, but instead of alternating between the two sides of the same ladder,

embellish by stitching through one side of one ladder, then one side of the next ladder (figure 4).

Try adding embellishments in groups around the tube, so there are beads between and within ladders, all in the same row.

To do this on a three-ladder tube, for example, bring your embellishment thread out of a bead on side 1 of ladder 1. Pick up your embellishment bead—or beads—and stitch down through the adjacent bead. Before you stitch up through the first bead in ladder 2, pick up your next embellishment bead or beads. Then stitch up through the first bead in ladder 2 (figure 5).

Repeat the above step on ladders 2 and 3, so that your embellishments reach all the way around the tube (figure 6).

Step up through ladder 1 and stitch down the ladder, bringing your thread out where you want to add the next group of embellishments around the tube.

NDEBELE START WITH VARYING BEAD SIZES

Using beads of different sizes in tubular herringbone stitch can cause the beadwork to bend in the direction of the smaller beads. The larger beads need a place to go and force the smaller beads aside. Use this technique to create three-dimensional shapes that vary from the standard tube.

To practice the start for the Ndebele method with two different sized beads, needle up 1 yard (91.4 cm) of thread. We'll use 8°s on ladder 1 and 11°s on ladder 2. Pick up four 8°s and four 11°s. Ladder 1 is made by the first four beads you pick up and ladder 2 by the second four beads you pick up.

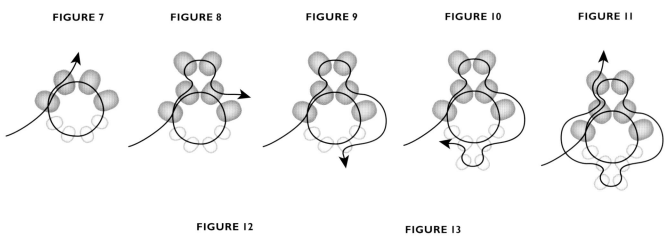

FIGURE 7   FIGURE 8   FIGURE 9   FIGURE 10   FIGURE 11

FIGURE 12   FIGURE 13

 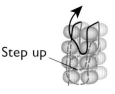

Step up

Stitch through the first two beads again (these should be 8°s) to form a ring (figure 7).

Pick up two 8°s and stitch through the next bead in the ring (figure 8). Skip over the next two beads in the ring (one 8° and one 11°) and stitch through the third (an 11°), as shown in figure 9.

Pick up two 11°s and stitch through the next bead in the ring (figure 10).

Skip over the next two beads (one 11° and one 8°) and stitch through the third (one 8°), then the bead after that to step up (figure 11).

If you pull on the working thread and tail thread, you'll see the two ladders. The 8°s are all on ladder 1 and the 11°s are all on ladder 2. From here on, you stitch pairs of 8°s onto ladder 1 and pairs of 11°s onto ladder 2, then step up at the end

of the row. After six or seven rows, you'll start to see the tube bending. The smaller beads will be on the inside of the curve. If you don't see a bend, you need to increase the tension of your beading thread. Pulling tight when using different sized beads is critical to get the correct shaping.

TWISTED TUBULAR HERRINGBONE STITCH

Twisted tubular herringbone stitch, or spiral herringbone, is just tubular herringbone stitch with a variation in the step up at the end of the round. There are a few different ways to do it, but I prefer the no-step-up method, which is very simple. After you complete a round and it comes time to step up, *don't* (figure 12).

That's it! If you have a long tube of spiral herringbone stitch to make, it's very easy because you don't have

to keep track of where the step up should happen.

You can use any number of ladders other than one. It's fine to start with either the laddering method or the Ndebele method. If you start with the Ndebele method, you'll end up with a base that actually includes a step up built into it (figure 13).

After you start the spiral, you can choose to pull out the first three rows if the visual inconsistency bothers you, but I usually find I don't even notice the difference between the rows.

PEYOTE STITCH

Peyote stitch involves picking up one bead, skipping over a bead, and stitching through the next bead. This creates a pattern that looks like a brick wall on its side. Peyote is very compatible with herringbone. Although only two projects in the

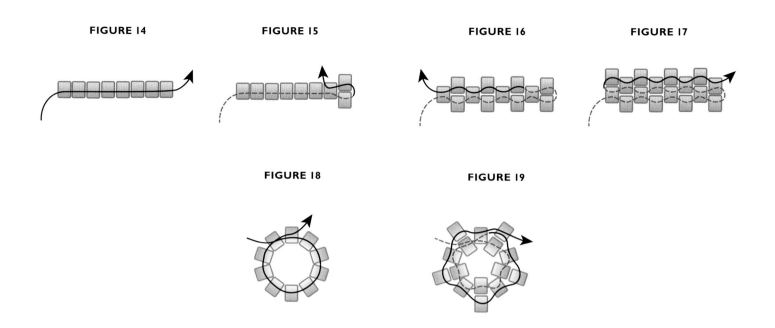

FIGURE 14   FIGURE 15   FIGURE 16   FIGURE 17

FIGURE 18   FIGURE 19

next two chapters incorporate peyote stitch, there are many great possibilities to explore.

Most peyote stitch starts with a row of beads strung onto the thread (figure 14).

Pick up one bead and stitch back through the second-to-last bead, not counting the one you just picked up (figure 15).

Pick up one bead, skip over one bead in the initial row, and stitch through the next. Repeat until you reach the end of the row (figure 16).

You now have three rows of peyote stitch. The initial *row* that you strung onto your thread becomes rows 1 and 2, and you just completed row 3.

Row 4 is much easier than row 3. Pick up a bead, then stitch through the next *up* bead, which is the next bead that's sticking out. Repeat until you reach the end of the row (figure 17).

TUBULAR PEYOTE STITCH

Peyote stitch in the round, better known as tubular peyote stitch, is used to create bezels that capture stones. To do it, you pick up the initial two rows of beads (an even number), and stitch through the first few beads again to form a loop (figure 18).

To stitch row 3—because the initial ring is already the first two rows—pick up one bead, skip over the next bead in the ring, and go through the next. Repeat all the way around the ring. After you add the last bead, step up by stitching through the first bead added in row 3. Continue to add beads with a step up at the end of each row until you reach the desired length (figure 19).

pod earrings

These pretty earrings are easier to make than they look! You use a modified four-ladder tubular herringbone stitch where you add beads between each ladder to create a pod-shaped form, which you then hang on the end of a line of beads.

YOU'LL NEED

Size 15° seed beads:

A, silver-lined black diamond AB, 5 g

B, matte higher metallic teal, 2 g

16 rose 2XAB crystal bicones, 3 mm

10 rose AB crystal bicones, 4 mm

Size 11° silver-plated cylinder beads, 1 g

2 silver-plated ear wires

Size 12 beading needles

Polyethylene or other strong beading thread

Scissors

Work surface

TECHNIQUES

Tubular Herringbone Stitch

Beads Between Ladders

DIMENSIONS

2⅛ inches (5.4 cm) long

DIFFICULTY LEVEL

Experienced beginner

OVERVIEW

You'll start with a base of four beads, upon which you'll build four ladders and continue to work in tubular herringbone stitch. After two rows, you'll begin adding beads between ladders and increase the bead counts between them as you work to create volume.

POD

Needle up a half wingspan of thread. Pick up four As and stitch through the first bead again to form a loop. Leave a 12-inch (30.5 cm) tail.

Row 2: Add one pair of As between each bead in the initial ring. After adding the fourth pair, step up through the first bead in the first pair added.

Row 3: Add pairs of As to each of the four ladders formed in row 2. Step up at the end of the row through the first bead in the first pair added.

Row 4: Add one pair of As to each ladder, and add one B when stitching from one ladder to the next. Step up at the end of the row through the first bead in the first pair added.

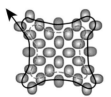

For rows 5 through 15, you will continue to always add one pair of As onto each ladder. The part of the row that varies is the number and type of bead added between each ladder. The following describes which beads to add between the ladders.

Row 5: Add two Bs between each ladder.
Row 6: Add three Bs between each ladder.
Row 7: Add one B, one 3-mm bicone, and one B between each ladder.

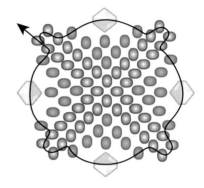

Row 8: Add one B, one 4-mm bicone, and one B between each ladder. ***Note:*** In rows 7 through 9, the bicones have a tendency to migrate to the inside of the form, so push them toward the outside of the form and keep a high thread tension as you work additional rows.
Row 9: Between each ladder, pick up one B, go through the 4-mm bicone from row 8, and pick up one B.

Row 10: Repeat row 7.
Row 11: Repeat row 6.
Row 12: Repeat row 5.
Row 13: Repeat row 4.
Row 14: Repeat row 3.
Row 15: Repeat row 3.
Row 16: Add one A atop each ladder.

Row 17: Stitch through all four beads added in row 16.

Secure your working thread in the beadwork and trim it.

EAR WIRE

Needle up your tail thread. Pick up one cylinder bead, one 4-mm bicone, one cylinder bead, four As, one cylinder bead, eight As, one cylinder bead, five As, and the loop of the ear wire. Skip over the last five As and stitch back through the rest of the beads you picked up. Stitch into the first row.

Reverse direction and repeat the thread path through the line of beads and the ear wire loop, then back into row 1. Secure your thread in the beadwork and trim it.

Repeat all steps to make a second earring.

trumpet lily earrings

These sweet earrings were inspired by the delicate and graceful shape of trumpet lily flowers. The project is a great introduction to tubular herringbone stitch and one that can be completed in about an hour.

YOU'LL NEED

Size 15° bronze-lined crystal AB round seed beads, 1 g

Size 11° silk light gold round seed beads, < 1 g

Size 8° matte metallic olive gold iris round seed beads, < 1 g

2 crystal drop pendants, 12 x 20 mm

2 gold-plated ear wires

Size 12 and 13 beading needles*

Beading thread

Scissors

Work surface

* You'll bead this project with size 12 needles, but keep size 13s on hand for the small holes in the bronze-lined 15° beads.

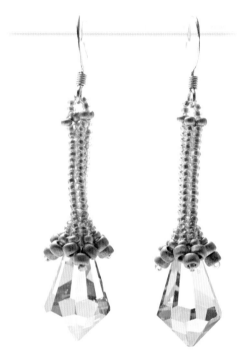

TECHNIQUES

Start Techniques

Two-Ladder Tubular Herringbone Stitch

Four-Ladder Tubular Herringbone Stitch

DIMENSIONS

2¼ inches (5.7 cm) long

DIFFICULTY LEVEL

Experienced beginner

OVERVIEW

You'll create the base of the earring using two-ladder tubular herringbone stitch and then convert it into four-ladder tubular herringbone stitch to widen the base. You'll add larger beads to flare out each ladder and nestle a drop between two opposite ladders. Lastly, you'll finish the top of the base and add the ear wire.

BASE

Rows 1–15: Needle up a wingspan of thread. Start a two-ladder tubular herringbone base with 15°s using either technique. Leave a tail 18 inches (45.7 cm) long.

Stitch a total of 15 rows of two-ladder tubular herringbone with 15°s.

Row 16: Add a pair of 15°s onto the first ladder, then add one 15° between the first and second ladder. Add a pair of 15°s onto the second ladder, and add one 15° between the second and first ladder.

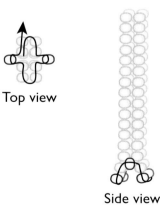

Top view

Side view

Row 17: Add a pair of 15°s onto the first ladder; add a pair of 15°s between the first and second ladder; add a pair of 15°s onto the second ladder; add a pair of 15°s between the second and first ladder. The pair of 15°s you just added between each ladder will serve as the base for two new ladders.

Side view

Top view

Row 18: Add a pair of 15°s onto each original ladder and onto the two new ladders between the original ladders.

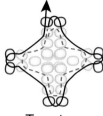 

Side view

Top view

Row 19: Add a pair of 11°s onto each ladder.

 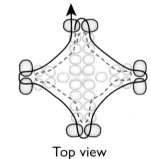

Side view

Top view

Row 20: Add a pair of 8°s onto each ladder.

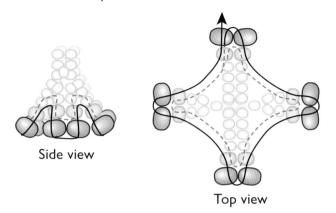

Side view

Top view

Row 21: Complete this row as embellishment—not herringbone stitch. Pick up one 8° and one 15°. Stitch back through the 8° and through the next 8° in the same ladder, then through the 11° that follows. Stitch down through the 11° and 8° in the next ladder.

Pick up one 8° and one 15°. Stitch back through the 8° and through the next 8° in the same ladder, then through the 11° that follows. Repeat this process with the remaining two ladders, then bring your thread out of an 11° on the inside of the base.

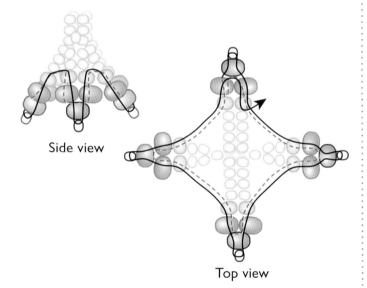

Side view

Top view

CRYSTAL DROP
Pick up the crystal drop and stitch directly across the tube, into an 11° on the opposite ladder. Stitch back through the crystal drop into an 11° on the original ladder. Repeat this thread path as many times as possible to secure the crystal drop snugly in the flared tube. Then secure your thread in the beadwork and trim it.

FINISH
Needle up the 18 inches (45.7 cm) of tail thread left when you started the base and bring the thread out of a 15° on the end—if it's not already emerging from one. Add a pair of 11°s to each ladder in two-ladder tubular herringbone stitch.

Pick up five 15°s and the bottom loop of the ear wire. Stitch into an 11° on the opposite ladder, then out of the other 11° on the same ladder. Stitch back through the five 15°s, then into the other 11° on the first ladder. Take up any slack and repeat the thread path if possible, then secure your thread in the beadwork and trim it.

variation

floral ring

The beauty of this ring is its simplicity. It uses herringbone stitch to pair crystal beads together around a focal pearl. This quick project can be completed in under a half hour!

OVERVIEW
You'll begin with a laddered base of beads in row 1, and then add rows in herringbone stitch. Next, you'll add beads between ladders to expand the beadwork outward and create the flower. Finally, you'll secure a pearl in the center of the beadwork and create a single ladder of herringbone from off of the base as the ring band.

BASE
1 Needle up a wingspan of thread and ladder together six 8°s, leaving an 18-inch (45.7 cm) tail.

2 Ladder the first bead to the last bead.

YOU'LL NEED

Size 8° seed beads, lavender-lined light amber, 1 g

Size 11° seed beads, permanent finish galvanized gold, 1 g

6 rose 2XAB crystal bicone beads, 4 mm

6 lavender crystal rivoli pendants, 6 mm

6 rose 2XAB crystal bicone beads, 3 mm

Lavender glass pearl, 6 mm

Size 10 or 11 beading needles

Polyethylene or other strong beading thread

Scissors

Work surface

TECHNIQUES

Start Techniques

Two-Ladder Tubular Herringbone Stitch

Four-Ladder Tubular Herringbone Stitch

DIMENSIONS

1³/₈ inches (3.5 cm) tall

DIFFICULTY LEVEL

Experienced beginner

Row 2: On each ladder, add one 11°, one 4-mm bicone, one 11°, one 4-mm bicone, and one 11°. Step up and exit through the first 4-mm bicone added.

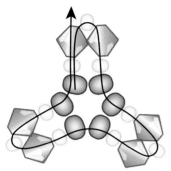

Row 3: On each ladder, add one rivoli pendant, one 11°, one 3-mm bicone, one 11°, and one rivoli pendant, skipping the middle 11° from the previous row. Step up and exit through the first 11° added.

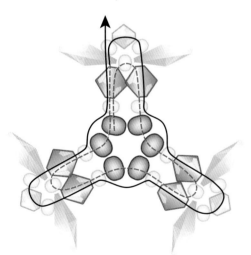

Row 4: Stitch through the rest of the beads added to ladder 1 in row 3. Pick up one 8° and stitch through the beads added to the next ladder in row 3. Repeat two times and stitch through to the first 8° added.

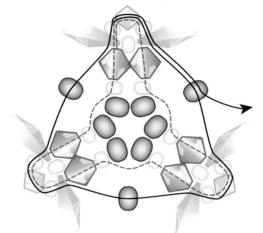

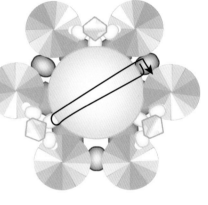

3 Pick up the 6-mm pearl, then stitch through the 11° across from the 8°, back through the pearl, and into the 8°. Secure your thread in the beadwork and trim it.

RING BAND

4 Needle up your tail thread, which should be emerging from an 8° in the base. Pick up two 11°s and stitch down through the adjacent 8°, then up through the first 8° and the first 11° added.

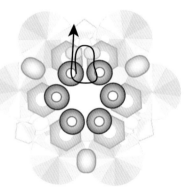

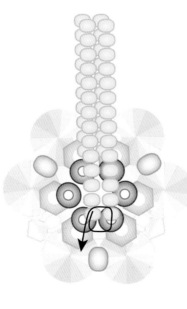

5 Use these two 11°s as a base to work single-ladder herringbone stitch until you have a ring band long enough to wrap around your finger. Ladder the last row to the pair of 8°s across from the starting pair. Secure your thread in the beadwork and trim it.

beaded capsule pendant

YOU'LL NEED

Size 11° silk bronze iris round seed beads, 2 g

Size 15° metallic bronze iris round seed beads, 2 g

3-mm drop seed beads:

>   A, translucent rust gold iris, 3 g

>   B, metallic olive gold iris, 6 g

Size 8° silk dark bronze iris round seed beads,
< 1 g

Crystal copper crystal rondelle, 12 x 9 mm

25 crystal copper crystal bicone beads, 4 mm

Size 12 beading needles

Beige beading thread

Scissors

Work surface

TECHNIQUES

Two-Ladder Tubular Herringbone Stitch

Single-Ladder Herringbone Stitch

Ladder Stitch

Peyote Stitch in the Round

Fringing

DIMENSIONS

1¼ x 3 inches (3.2 x 7.6 cm)

DIFFICULTY LEVEL

Intermediate

This project is an exercise in two-ladder herringbone stitch using different sized beads at different places in the design to create three-dimensionality. The six-fold symmetry and rounded shape of the beaded pendant make it look very organic. Two of these pendants could also make a very interesting pair of earrings!

See note on page 40 about selecting magatamas.

OVERVIEW

The pendant "cage" is made from two-ladder herringbone stitch built from a peyote stitch base. The cage's shape is created by changing beads on each herringbone ladder. The freely turning rondelle is suspended in the center of the cage and attached to the bail.

BASE

1 Needle up 1 yard (91.4 cm) of thread and string on twelve 11°s. Leave just enough of a tail to weave into the beadwork later and secure. Go through the first two beads again to form a loop.

2 Add three rounds of 11°s in peyote stitch in the round, stepping up after each round and tightening your thread. Your beadwork should be shaping into a small cylinder. Add one round of 15°s. After this round, step down three rounds, bringing your thread out of the beadwork on the outside of the cylinder in the second round.

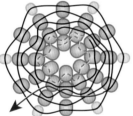

3 Pick up two 15°s, then stitch through the next 11° in the round. Continue to add pairs of 15°s between every 11° in the round. After the sixth pair, stitch up two rounds in the cylinder, bringing your thread out on the outside of the cylinder.

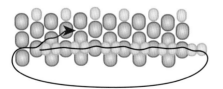

4 Working in the 11° round directly beneath the 15° round, add pairs of 11°s between every bead in the round. Then step up into the first bead of the first pair added after you complete the round.

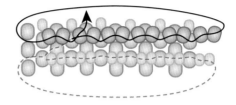

ARMS

5 The arms that form the cage part of the pendant extend out of the peyote stitch cylinder. Your thread should be emerging from the first bead of the first pair of 11°s you added to the outside of the cylinder, and there should be a pair of 15°s directly beneath the pair of 11°s. You will use the pair of 11°s and the pair of 15°s as the base for the two ladders in two-ladder tubular herringbone stitch. The pair of 11°s will be the start of one ladder, and the pair of 15°s will be the start of the other. Beads added in steps 3 and 4 become row 1.

Rows 2–6: Add five rows of two-ladder herringbone stitch, adding 11°s onto the initial pair of 11°s, and 15°s onto the initial pair of 15°s.

Rows 7–10: Add As onto the 11° ladder and 15°s onto the 15° ladder.

Rows 11–16: Add 11°s onto the 11° ladder and 15°s onto the 15° ladder.

Rows 17–24: Add 15°s onto the 11° ladder and Bs onto the 15° ladder. Then add a single B on the end of the 3-mm drop ladder.

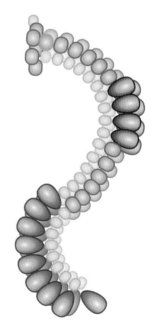

6 Secure your thread in the beadwork and trim it. To create the other arms, start a new half wingspan of thread within the peyote stitch base and bring it out of another 11° pair added to the base in step 4. Create each arm the same as the first. With all the arms but one, when finished, secure your thread in the beadwork and trim it. Leave the thread hanging on one arm for later.

BAIL AND CAPSULE CENTER

7 Ladder together four 11°s, then ladder the first to the last so you have a square of four 11°s with the holes all oriented in the same direction.

8 Add 18 rows of 11°s in single-ladder herringbone stitch off of two adjacent beads in the four-bead base.

9 Zip the end of the ladder to the other two 11°s in the four-bead base by adding them as your next stitch.

Drop 1: From the start of the arms toward their ends, stitch through the center of the peyote stitch base and pick up three 8°s. Pick up the rondelle, eight 8°s, four 15°s, one bicone, one 15°, one bicone, one 15°, one bicone, and four 15°s. Skip the last three 15°s, then go back through the rest of the 15°s and bicones just added, bringing your thread out before the first 8°. Take up any slack in the thread.

Drop 2: Pick up seven 15°s, one bicone, one 15°, one bicone, one 15°, one bicone, one 15°, one bicone, one 15°, one bicone, and four 15°s. Skip the last three 15°s, then go back through the rest of the beads just added, bringing your thread out before the 8°.

Drop 3: Pick up one 15°, one bicone, one 15°, one bicone, one 15°, one bicone, one 15°, one bicone, and four 15°s. Skip the last three 15°s and go back through the rest of the beads just added, then through one 8°.

Drop 5: Pick up two 15°s, one bicone, one 15°, one bicone, one 15°, one bicone, one 15°, one bicone, one 15°, one bicone, and four 15°s.

Skip the last three 15°s and go back through the rest of the beads added, then through the next 8°s, the rondelle, and the next three 8°s, then stitch through the bail. Repeat the thread path through the capsule center and the first drop to reinforce the connection. Then secure your thread in the beadwork and trim it.

Drop 4: Pick up three 15°s, one bicone, one 15°, one bicone, one 15°, one bicone, one 15°, one bicone, one 15°, one bicone, one 15°, one bicone, and four 15°s. Skip the last three 15°s and go back through the rest of the beads added, then through the next 8°.

FINISH

10 Pick up the thread you left hanging on one of the arms. Stitch through the beadwork and bring your thread out of a B in the third row that contains Bs (row 19). Stitch this B to the closest B in row 19 on the adjacent arm.

Then weave through to the next B and stitch it to the B in row 19 on the adjacent arm. Repeat all around the pendant so all six arms are attached at row 19.

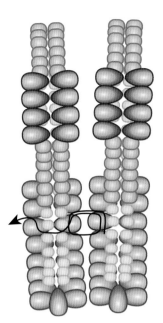

transcription bracelet

The shape of this bracelet reminds me of the way DNA wraps around the proteins called histones in the nucleus of a cell in order to stay untangled yet save space. Like DNA itself, this bracelet is helical and rhythmic, rigidly structured but with soft curves. I've named it for a part of the process of replicating DNA. Once a science geek, always a science geek!

Bracelet length	Number of pearls
6 inches (15.2 cm)	11
6½ inches (16.5 cm)	12
7 inches (17.8 cm)	13
7½ inches (19 cm)	14
8 inches (20.3 cm)	15

See the box on page 40 concerning magatamas.

YOU'LL NEED

Size 15° gold-lined crystal AB round seed beads, 3 g

Size 11° silver-lined topaz AB round seed beads, 5 g

3.4-mm metallic purple magatama drop beads, 3 g

Size 6° matte metallic cabernet round seed beads, 7 g

Gold glass pearls, 10 mm*

Purple crystal rivoli, 18 mm

Size 12 beading needles

Gold nylon thread or crystal polyethylene

Scissors

Beading surface

*This amount varies depending on how long of a bracelet you want to make. See box at left.

TECHNIQUES

Ndebele Start with Varying Bead Sizes

Two-Ladder Tubular Herringbone Stitch

Single-Ladder Herringbone Stitch

Bezel

DIMENSIONS

7½ inches (19 cm) long

DIFFICULTY LEVEL

Intermediate

OVERVIEW

First, you'll create the base of this bracelet in two-ladder tubular herringbone stitch. You'll then add pearls between sections of the base to hold the structure together in an orderly fashion. You'll create a beaded bezel for the rivoli using the same technique as the bracelet base. You'll attach this bezeled stone to one end of the bracelet to act as a button and create a beaded loop using single-ladder herringbone stitch on the other end of the bracelet.

BASE

1 Create the base as follows.

Rows 1–3: Needle up a wingspan of thread and start a two-ladder tube of herringbone stitch with the Ndebele start method (page 60) using 15°s for one ladder and 11°s for the other; leave an 18-inch (45.7 cm) tail.

Row 4: Add a row with 11°s on the 11° ladder and 15°s on the 15° ladder.

Row 5: Add a pair of drop beads on the 11° ladder and a pair of 15°s on the 15° ladder.

Row 6: Add a pair of 6°s on the 11° ladder and a pair of 15°s on the 15° ladder.

Row 7: Repeat row 5.

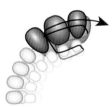

Row 8-11: Add four rows with 11°s on the 11° ladder and 15°s on the 15° ladder.

2 Stitch repeats of rows 5–11. For a 6-inch (15.2 cm) bracelet, do 22 total repeats of the pattern (counting the first sequence). For bracelets 6½ inches (16.5 cm), 7 inches (17.8 cm), 7½ inches (19 cm), or 8 inches (20.3 cm) long, do 24 repeats, 26 repeats, 28 repeats, or 30 repeats, respectively. When you've completed the repeats, secure your thread in the beadwork and trim it.

PEARLS

3 Start a new doubled thread and secure it close to the beginning of the bracelet base. Bring your thread out of an 11° in the second row. Pick up one 15°, then stitch through the base between the 11°s in rows 2 and 3, then through the 15° ladder between rows 2 and 3. You should not be stitching through any beads, just directly through the base between beads.

Pick up one pearl, and then stitch through the base in the second repeat, between the second and third rows. Again, do not stitch through any beads, just directly through the base, between the beads. Pick up one 15°, then stitch back through the base and take up any slack in your thread.

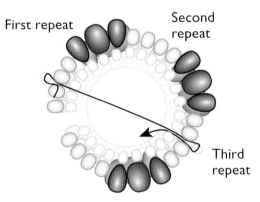

First repeat

Second repeat

Third repeat

4 Pick up another pearl, stitch through the base in the fourth repeat and between the second and third rows. Pick up one 15°, then stitch back through the base between the second and third rows.

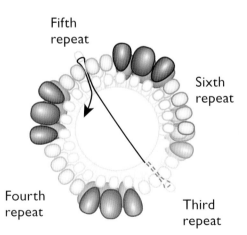

Fifth repeat

Sixth repeat

Fourth repeat

Third repeat

5 Continue attaching pearls between the odd rows along the entire length of the bracelet base. When you're finished, weave through to the end of the base and bring the thread out of one of the 11°s in the last row. Leave this thread hanging for attachment of the rivoli bezel-button later.

RIVOLI BEZEL
6 Stitch 48 rows of two-ladder tubular herringbone beginning with the Ndebele start method (page 60). Use 15°s on one ladder and 11°s on the other ladder for every row. After the 48th row, stitch as though the first row is the next set of beads you will add to do a 49th row. This will zip the two ends together for a seamless connection and keep the thread path consistent.

7 Bring your thread out of a 15° on the inside of the bezel. For this step you will work on just one side of the 15° ladder. Pick up eight 15°s, one drop bead, and eight 15°s. Stitch through the twelfth 15° on the inside of the bezel from the one in which you started, in the same direction, and stitch back through the last eight 15°s added.

8 Pick up one drop bead and eight 15°s. Stitch through the twelfth 15° on the inside of the bezel from the one to which the last group of eight 15°s is attached and stitch back through the last eight 15°s added.

9 Repeat step 8. Pick up one drop bead, and stitch through the first eight 15°s added. Stitch through the twelfth 15° on the inside of the bezel from the one to which the last group of eight 15°s is attached.

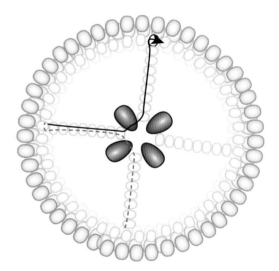

10 Stitch back through the last eight 15°s, through each of the four drop beads, and through the second group of eight 15°s added and into the beadwork of the bezel.

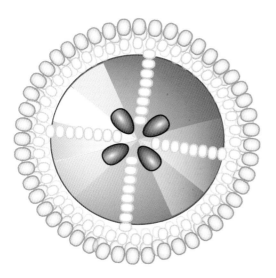

11 Bring your thread out of a 15° on the other side of the 15° ladder. Place the rivoli in the bezel, back side against the beadwork last added.

12 Hold the rivoli in place while you add the same pattern of beadwork to the front side of the bezel that you just added to the back side. Then secure your thread in the beadwork and trim it.

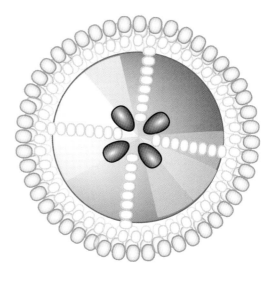

CLOSURE
13 Needle up your hanging thread on the end of the bracelet base. Pick up eight 11°s and stitch through three drop beads on the back of the rivoli bezel in a circle. Pick up eight 11°s and stitch into the other large bead in the last row of the bracelet base. Repeat the thread path several times to reinforce the connection.

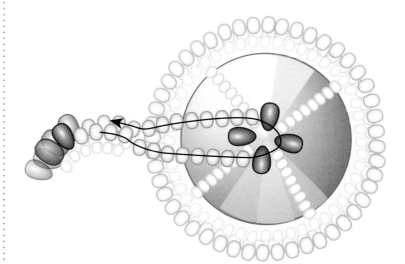

14 Start a new thread at the beginning of the bracelet base and bring it out of an 11°. Use single-ladder herringbone stitch to add four rows of 11°s, one row of drop beads, one row of 6°s, and one row of drop beads. This is one repeat of the pattern for the toggle loop.

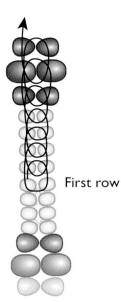

First row

Front of the button

Back of the button

15 Repeat step 14 four more times and finish four more rows of 11°s. Zip the end of the loop to the 15° ladder on the bracelet base by stitching as though the first row of 15°s is the next pair of beads you will pick up for your single-ladder herringbone stitch. Then stitch as though the second row of 15°s in the base is the next pair of beads you'll pick up. This will create a consistent thread path while turning the single-ladder herringbone into a loop.

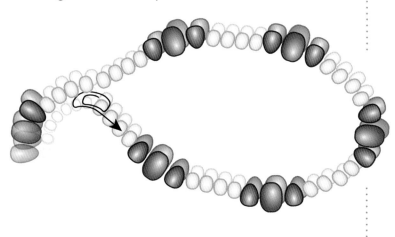

16 Secure your thread in the beadwork and trim it.

willow lariat

Size 13° stable finish light gold Czech charlotte seed beads, 50 g

24 green amethyst briolette pendants, 10 x 10 mm

Size 12 beading needles

Polyethylene or other strong beading thread

Scissors

Work surface

TECHNIQUES

Ndebele Start

Modified Two-Ladder Tubular Herringbone Stitch

DIMENSIONS

30 inches (76.2 cm) long

DIFFICULTY LEVEL

Intermediate

By using a modified two-ladder twisted tubular herringbone stitch and small charlotte beads, you can create this delicate, four-sided open-weave necklace.

OVERVIEW

You'll begin with a base that is a modified version of the Ndebele start method (page 50) and then work each row of the herringbone rope off of that base. Once the rope is the length you desire, accounting for knotting or twisting depending on how you'll wear the necklace, add embellishments to each end.

BASE

You'll use the 13°s for the lariat. Needle up a wingspan of thread and pick up 14 beads. Go through the first three beads again to form a loop, leaving a tail 18 inches (45.7 cm) long.

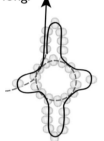

Pick up seven beads, skip over the next bead in the loop, and pass through the two after that. Pick up one bead, skip over the next two in the loop, and pass through the two after that. Pick up seven beads, skip over the next bead in the loop, and go through the two after that. Pick up one bead, skip over the next two, and go through the two after that, then step up through the first three beads added in this step. You'll see the two ladders form when you pull the threads tight.

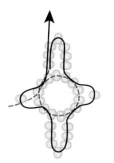

CHAIN

Pick up seven beads, skip the middle bead from the previous row, and stitch down through two beads. Pick up one bead—between the two ladders—and looking at the top seven-bead group in the second ladder, stitch up through the second and third beads.

Pick up seven beads, skip over the middle bead, and stitch through the next two. Pick up one bead, and then stitch up through the second and third beads in the top seven-bead group on the first ladder. This is *not* a step up—you will get a twisted tube.

Repeat the last step until your lariat is the desired length.

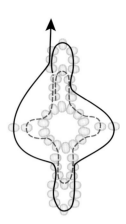

EMBELLISHMENTS

Needle up your tail thread. Pick up three beads, one briolette, and three beads. Stitch up through the three bottom beads on the other ladder, then through the nearest middle bead and down through the other three beads in the ladder. Pick up three beads, then stitch back through the briolette and pick up three beads. Stitch up through the three beads on the other side of the other ladder.

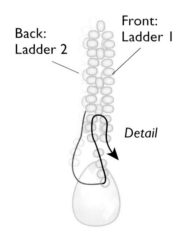

Back:
Ladder 2

Front:
Ladder I

Detail

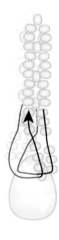

Now, add all the remaining embellishments at this end of the lariat to the side of the chain, which is between the two ladders. The seventh through 12th embellishments are more spaced out than the first through sixth.

Embellishments 2–6: Your thread is now emerging from one side of one of the ladders. Pick up three beads, one briolette, and three beads. Stitch up through six beads in the nearest side of the other ladder.

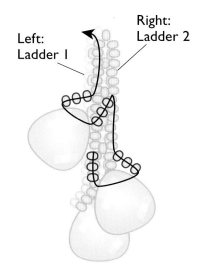

Embellishments 7–12: Pick up three beads, one briolette, and three beads. Stitch up through nine beads in the nearest side of the other ladder. Secure your thread in the beadwork and trim it.

Needle up your working thread and repeat the 12 embellishments on the second end of the chain. Then secure your thread in the beadwork and trim it.

opulent beaded bead

YOU'LL NEED

Size 11° silk matte olive
    seed beads, 1 g

3.4-mm drop magatama seed beads:

    A, transparent sunset gold luster,
    18 pieces

    B, transparent olive gold luster,
    18 pieces

9 tan freshwater pearls, 4 to 5 mm

18 bronze glass pearls, 4 mm

9 chrysolite crystal rondelles,
    4 x 6 mm

Size 10 or 11 beading needles

Polyethylene or other strong beading
    thread

Scissors

Work surface

TECHNIQUES

Three-Ladder Tubular Herringbone
    Stitch

Ladder Stitch

DIMENSIONS

¼ x 1¼ inches (6 mm x 3.2 cm)

DIFFICULTY

Advanced

Use tubular herringbone stitch to create a solid encrusted beaded bead that can be used as a spacer or focal point. By stepping up and alternating the beads in each row, you get a rich, embellished look in only one step.

See note on page 40 about choosing magatamas.

OVERVIEW

You'll start with a laddered base of the beads in row 1, then add row 2 in herringbone stitch. Continue adding rows of herringbone stitch, alternating the pattern in each row until you reach the 18th row. Invisibly join the last row to the first row to create a seamless connection and finish the bead.

BASE

1 Ladder together the following beads, one at a time: 11°, 11°, 11°, A, freshwater pearl, and A.

2 Ladder the last bead to the first bead.

Row 2: Use the first laddered row as the base for three-ladder tubular herringbone stitch. Add one 11° and one B to the first pair of beads. Add one glass pearl and one rondelle to the second pair of beads. Add one glass pearl and one B to the third pair of beads. Step up through two beads. The diagram shows the exploded view of the ladders for clarity.

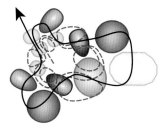

Row 3: Add two 11°s to ladder 1. Add one A and one freshwater pearl to ladder 2. Add one A and one 11° to ladder 3.

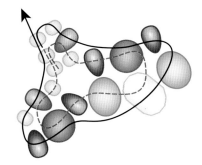

Rows 4–18: For the even rows, add the beads used in row 2. For the odd rows, add the beads used in row 3. Remember to step up at the end of each row.

FINISH

3 To seamlessly join the last row to the first row, stitch through the beads in row 1 as if you're adding them to create row 19. Step up at the end of the *row*. This will create a thread path identical to the rest of the beadwork so you will not see the seam. If your beadwork is loose and you can see the seam, repeat the thread path once more and pull tightly to close the gap between the first and last rows.

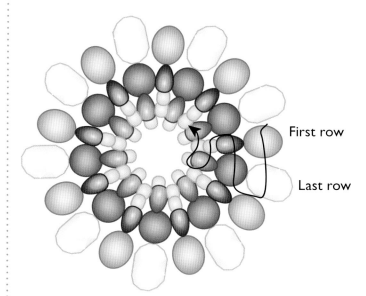

First row

Last row

victorian elegance necklace

Despite its complicated look, this necklace uses only two techniques. The visual richness and complexity come from the variety of colors, finishes, and sizes of beads. This project is an excellent exercise in how color and movement affect the overall look and feel of a piece of jewelry.

OVERVIEW

You'll create a number of curved units individually, which you'll then stitch together to create the completed necklace. The longer your necklace, the more curved units you'll make. You'll also create a beaded toggle bar and loop, which serve as a closure that complements the necklace perfectly. Keep the thread tension high when you stitch in two-ladder herringbone in this project, because this will create solid curved units that will hold their shape nicely.

YOU'LL NEED

Size 8° round seed beads:

    A, noir-lined amber AB, 9 g

    B, silk metallic gold iris, 9 g

    C, silk dark bronze iris, 1 g

Size 11° silk dark bronze iris round seed beads, 9 g

#3 translucent fuchsia gold luster twisted bugles, 2 g

28 dusty rose fire-polished glass rounds, 4 mm

Size 15° metallic dark copper round seed beads, 1 g

15-mm matte translucent fuchsia gold luster twisted bugles, 18 g

91 crystal 2XAB crystal bicone beads, 4 mm

3.4-mm translucent rust gold luster magatama drop beads, 5 g

Size 12 beading needles

Polyethylene beading thread

Beige nylon thread

Scissors

Work surface

• • • • • • • • • • • • • • • • • •

TECHNIQUES

Start Techniques

Two-Ladder Tubular Herringbone Stitch

Embellishing

• • • • • • • • • • • • • • • • • •

DIMENSIONS

13 inches (33 cm) long

• • • • • • • • • • • • • • • • • •

DIFFICULTY LEVEL

Advanced

Check the box on page 40 for information on selecting magatamas.

CURVED UNITS

Rows 1–3: Needle up a wingspan of thread. Create a basic two-ladder herringbone stitch base with 8° As on one ladder and 11°s on the other, using either method (pages 49 or 50). Leave a tail 24 inches (61 cm) long.

Rows 4–6: After your initial three-row base, stitch three more identical rows with As on the same ladder and 11°s on the other ladder.

Rows 7–10: Add Bs on the 8° ladder and 11°s on the 11° ladder.

Rows 11–16: Add As on the 8° ladder and 11°s on the 11° ladder. A significant curve will arise in the tube at this point. If your beadwork is loose and the curve is less pronounced than you'd like, you can stitch down and back through the lines of 11°s and pull tight to snug up the curve.

You'll stitch the herringbone ladders with polyethylene beading thread for strength. The nylon thread should be used to add the fringe drops for a supple drape.

Row 17: Add a pair of 11°s to the 8° ladder and a pair of drop beads to the 11° ladder.

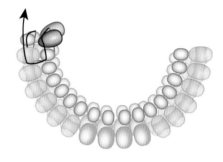

BUGLE DROPS

You'll work within one column of beads in the 8° ladder to add all the bugle drops. Stitch back four rows and bring your thread out of the 8° in row 13. After adding each sequence of beads, skip the 15° and stitch back through the beads just added and through the 8° in the next row.

Drop 1: Add one 11°, one #3 bugle, two 11°s, one A, one fire-polished round, one B, and one 15°.

Drop 2: Add one 11°, one 15-mm bugle, one B, one bicone, one B, and one 15°.

Drop 3: Add two 11°s, one 15-mm bugle, one B, one bicone, one B, and one 15°.

Drop 4: Add three 11°s, one 15-mm bugle, one B, one bicone, one B, and one 15°.

Drop 5: Repeat drop 4.

Drop 6: Repeat drop 4.

Drop 7: Repeat drop 3.

Drop 8: Repeat drop 2. Stitch through the remaining 8°s in the same side of the 8° ladder, bringing your thread out of the end of the tube. Add a pair of 11°s to the 8° ladder and a pair of drop beads to the 11° ladder, then secure your thread in the beadwork and trim it.

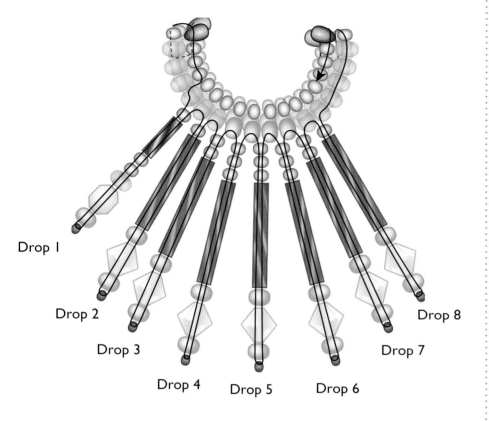

Drop 1

Drop 2

Drop 3

Drop 4   Drop 5   Drop 6

Drop 7

Drop 8

DROP BEAD FRINGE

To add the drop beads, you will *not* stitch through 8°s but through loops of thread between 8° rows on the outside of the curved tube. Needle up your hanging thread and weave down through the beadwork, bringing your thread out of an 8° in row 5. Pick up one drop bead, then catch the thread that spans between pairs of 8°s in the sixth and seventh rows.

This will allow the drop bead to sit on top of and between the 8°s in row 6. Add four more drop beads using this method. Then pick up a sixth drop bead and stitch into an 8° in row 12, then through the column of beads in rows 13 through 17, bringing your thread out of an 11° on the end.

For a necklace 13 inches (33 cm) long, make 13 of these units. For each additional inch (2.5 cm) of length desired, make one additional unit. Take care when adding the drop bead fringe to stitch them in exactly the same manner for each unit, so drop 1 is oriented the same way on each unit relative to the drop bead fringe.

Top view
(bugle drops omitted)

CONNECT THE UNITS

Align two units so they're identical, making sure that drop 1 is on the same side of each unit. This is the front side. Align the first three rows of one unit with the last three rows of the other. Needle up the hanging thread located closest to the junction between the two units. Pick up one fire-polished round and one 15°. Stitch into 8°s in the second row from the end, laddering them together and repeating with the third rows from the end in each unit. Then stitch down through two more 8°s, bringing your thread out of an 8° in the fourth row of 8°s. There should *not* be a drop 1 present here on the unit from which your thread is emerging. The drop 1 belonging to this unit should be on the other end of the tube.

Pick up one 11° and one #3 bugle. Stitch into drop 1 on the other unit after the #3 bugle, through two 11°s, an A, a fire-polished round, a B, and a 15°. Stitch back up through one B, one fire-polished round, one A, and two 11°s. Stitch through the bugle that was already part of drop 1 and the following 11°. Stitch through the beadwork and bring your thread out of the 11° on the end that isn't already attached to the fire-polished round.

Repeat this entire process, working in the back side of the 8° ladder, to double up the connection between the units and thread through the now shared drop 1.

Repeat this process to connect each additional unit.

CLOSURE

1 To create the toggle loop, needle up a wingspan of thread and start a two-ladder tubular herringbone base using either method (pages 49 or 50) with As on one ladder and 11°s on the other ladder.

Counting the base rows, stitch three rows with As on the 8° ladder and 11°s on the 11° ladder. Stitch four rows with Bs on the 8° ladder and 11°s on the 11° ladder. Stitch seven rows with As on the 8° ladder and 11°s on the 11° ladder. Stitch four rows with Bs on the 8° ladder and 11°s on the 11° ladder. Stitch three rows with As on the 8° ladder and 11°s on the 11° ladder. You should have a solid ring after connecting the end of the ring to the beginning by picking up each bead pair in the first row as if you're adding an additional two-ladder tubular herringbone stitch row.

2 Bring your thread out through the exterior of the ring. Ladder two 8°s in the toggle ring to two 8°s on the end necklace unit. Then repeat this laddering on the other side of the 8° ladder in the toggle ring and the other side of the 8° ladder in the end necklace unit.

3 Needle up 1 yard (91.4 cm) of thread. Ladder together four Cs, leaving an 18-inch (45.7 cm) tail.

4 Bring the fourth bead and the first bead together and ladder them together. You'll use this square of four beads as a base for two-ladder tubular herringbone stitch to create your toggle bar.

5 Stitch seven rows of two-ladder tubular herringbone stitch with Cs, for a total of eight rows. Add a ninth row using drop beads. Needle up the tail thread and add a row of drop beads to the first row.

6 On each end of the toggle bar, pick up one fire-polished round and one 15° and then stitch back through the fire-polished round and into a different end bead. Bring your thread out of a third end bead and repeat the thread path through the fire-polished round and the 15°, then stitch into the fourth end bead, so each end bead is connected to the fire-polished round.

Repeat this embellishment on the other end of the toggle bar. Secure the shorter thread within the beadwork and trim it. With your longer thread, weave through the toggle bar and bring the thread out of the middle.

7 Pick up seven 11°s and stitch through the open-end necklace unit—close to the end—then catch threads as you reverse direction and stitch back through the seven 11°s and into the middle of the toggle bar. Repeat this thread path as many time as possible to strengthen the connection, because this will be a point of high stress. Then secure your thread in the beadwork and trim it.

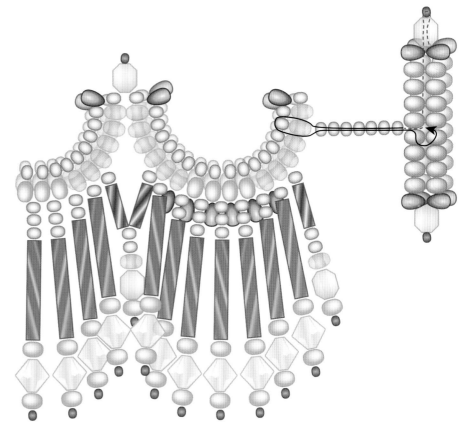

6

bezeled stones

· · · · · · · · · · · · · · ·

The jewelry projects in this chapter use stones as focal points. So how do you capture them in your beadwork? I'll show you three different methods.

FAUX BEZEL

With large focal beads, an easy way to fake the look of a captured stone is to shape a piece of herringbone that mimics the outer shape of your focal bead. The beadwork wraps around the outer edge of the focal bead, giving the appearance of a bezel, while the thread passing through the bead holds it securely in place.

FIGURE I

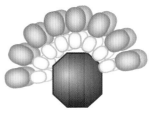

To do this, create a curved two-ladder tube of herringbone stitch using one size of beads on ladder 1 and a different size of beads on ladder 2. As you stitch the tube, wrap it around the bead you want to capture to measure its length against the bead perimeter (figure 1).

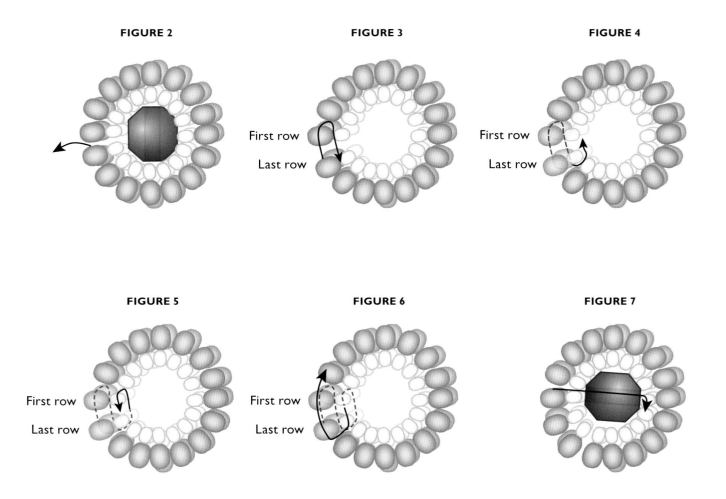

FIGURE 2

FIGURE 3

First row

Last row

FIGURE 4

First row

Last row

FIGURE 5

First row

Last row

FIGURE 6

First row

Last row

FIGURE 7

When you've stitched a long enough tube to reach around the entire bead, stop adding rows (figure 2).

Now make a seamless join from the last row to the first row, using the same type of thread path used to add the beads in each row. The best way to get the thread path correct is to stitch as though you're adding another row onto the tube, without picking up any new beads. Instead, use the beads in row 1 as the beads you're adding in this last row.

Your thread is emerging from the first bead in ladder 1 in the last row, after you completed your step up. Stitch up through the first bead in ladder 1, row 1, then back through the second bead in ladder 1, row 1, and through the second bead in ladder 1 in the last row (figure 3).

Stitch up through the first bead in the last row in ladder 2 (figure 4).

Stitch up through the first bead in ladder 2, row 1, then back through the second bead in ladder 2, row 1 (figure 5).

Stitch through the second bead in ladder 2 in the last row, then up through the first bead in ladder 1 in the last row, and through the first bead in ladder 1, row 1 (figure 6).

This last part is equivalent to doing a step up at the end of the row. Pull your thread tight and the two tube ends should come seamlessly together. If your thread is slack and you can't get it to tighten up, or if you notice a gap between the first and last rows, repeat the thread path used to join the two rows, pulling tightly as you stitch.

To add your bead into the middle of the circular tube you created, simply stitch through the bead hole and into a bead on the opposite side of the tube, repeating the thread path to secure the bead (figure 7).

FIGURE 8

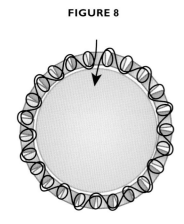

FIGURE 9

BEZEL

In this technique, you create a base that reaches all the way around the equator of the stone, then stitch tubular herringbone off of it. Always begin the base with ladder stitch (page 49); avoid the Ndebele method.

Choose your bead sizes carefully so that you have an even number of beads laddered together in the first row to reach around the perimeter of the stone (figure 8).

To secure the stone, decrease the bead sizes in subsequent rows of beads. The beadwork will cup and create a bezel to hold your stone in place (figure 9).

The projects in this chapter that have bezeled stones—the Da Vinci Earrings, Spellbound Bracelet, and Descending Scales Pendant—specify bead sizes, as well as the number of rows to stitch, so you can become acquainted with bead sizes that work with this technique.

CAPTURING STONES WITH OTHER STITCHES

Tubular peyote stitch (page 62) is useful for capturing stones. Much as with herringbone, decreasing the size of the beads as you stitch causes the beadwork to cup around the stone. Add these bezeled stones to a project made of herringbone by stitching the individual parts of the project together. Sinusoidal Necklace uses this method to incorporate stones into a herringbone project.

This is an example of thinking about beadwork as multiple levels of structure. In more advanced projects, a number of parts are created separately, and then stitched together. The first level of structure is the stitch or stitches used to create the individual parts. The next level consists of arranging the parts into the piece of jewelry. Two people could start with the exact same parts and arrange them differently to create unique designs.

Thinking of design in multiple levels opens up a whole world of design possibilities. I encourage you to take what you've learned in these pages to create your own jewelry with multiple levels of structure.

descending scales pendant

YOU'LL NEED

YOU'LL NEED

Size 8° matte metallic olive gold iris round seed beads, 3 g

Size 11° silk dark bronze iris round seed beads, 1 g

Size 15° metallic purple gold iris round seed beads, 1 g

Oval crystal stone, 22 x 30 mm

Size 10 to 12 beading needles

Polyethylene or other strong beading thread

Scissors

Work surface

TECHNIQUES

Ladder Stitch

Tubular Herringbone Stitch

Flat Herringbone Stitch

DIMENSIONS

1 1/8 x 2 inches (2.7 x 5.1 cm)

DIFFICULTY LEVEL

Experienced beginner

This project offers an alternative way to bezel an oval stone. The bezel provides opportunities for various embellishments because of the orientation of the bead holes, which radiate from the stone to the outside of the bezel. Use this project as a base to experiment with decorations! The name of the pendant is a play on words, based both on the decreasing size of the beads used to capture the stone and on the pendant's scaly appearance.

OVERVIEW

Begin by laddering together 8°s for the outside edge of the bezel. You'll then build both the front and the back of the bezel from the inside of the 8° ring using tubular herringbone stitch. Lastly, you'll add a bail at the top of the bezel in flat herringbone.

BASE

Needle up a wingspan of thread. Leave a 6-inch (15.2 cm) tail to secure in the beadwork later, and ladder together thirty-two 8°s. Ladder together the first 8° to the last 8° so that you have a ring with the bead holes oriented from outside to inside and your thread emerges on the inside.

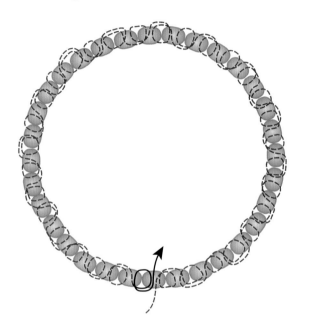

BEZEL BACK

Row 2: Add pairs of 11°s in tubular herringbone stitch onto each pair of 8°s on the inside of the ring. Step up at the end of the round.

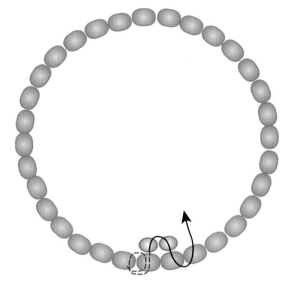

Row 3: Add pairs of 11°s. Step up at the end of the round.

Row 4: Do three stitches using 15°s, five stitches using 11°s, three stitches using 15°s, and five stitches using 11°s. Step up at the end of the round, then weave down to the 8° round and reverse direction so your thread is emerging from an 8° on the inside.

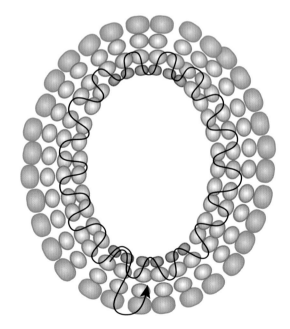

BEZEL FRONT

Put your oval stone in the bezel, front side up. Hold it in place as you work.

Row 5: Continuing in tubular herringbone, add pairs of 11°s onto each pair of 8°s. Step up at the end of the round.

Row 6: Add all 15°s. After you step up at the end of the round, weave through the beadwork to one of the far sides of the bezel, where the bail will be added. You will add four 8°s centered on this end of the bezel for the bail, so make sure your thread is emerging from the first of the four 8°s (red dots).

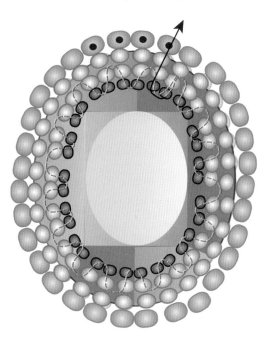

BAIL

Stitch two stitches of flat herringbone using 8°s along the outside of the bezel. Turn around and step up through the last bead added at the end of the row.

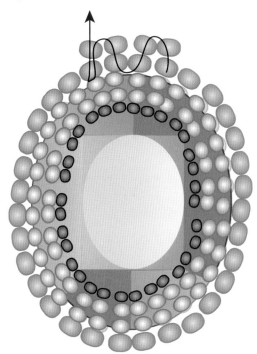

Stitch 11 rows total with 8°s. Then zip the last row to the base row of 8°s in the bezel by stitching through them with the flat herringbone stitch thread path.

Secure all your hanging threads in the beadwork and trim them.

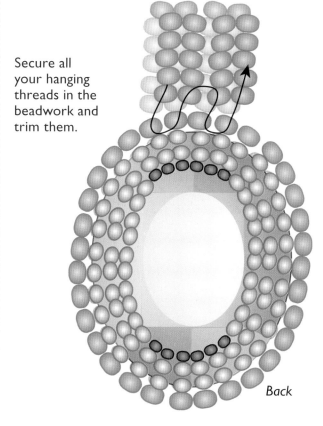

Back

spellbound bracelet

Each cabochon is captured with a bezel created with tubular herringbone stitch. By incorporating increasingly smaller bead sizes, you can form a cupped shape that holds the cabochon perfectly in place.

YOU'LL NEED

Size 8° matte black round seed beads, 12 g

Size 11° black/blue dichroic cylinder beads, 6 g

Size 13° special galvanized gold cut seed beads, 1 g

7 sky-blue round Czech glass cabochons, 13 mm

12 jet AB fire-polished rounds, 4 mm

Jet AB glass rondelle, 2.5 x 6 mm

Size 12 beading needles

Black beading thread

Scissors

Work surface

TECHNIQUES

Ladder Stitch

Bezel

Tubular Herringbone Stitch

DIMENSIONS

6½ inches (16.5 cm) long

DIFFICULTY LEVEL

Experienced beginner

OVERVIEW

You'll start each bezel by laddering together pairs of 8°s and working herringbone stitch off of this base. After bezeling the stones, you'll connect them with fire-polished rounds to create a chain-like assembly. You'll create a simple closure using a loop of thread and a rondelle as a button.

BASE

1 Needle up a wingspan of thread. Leaving a 6-inch (15.2 cm) tail to weave into the beadwork later and secure, pick up two 8°s, one 11°, and two 8°s. Go through all the beads again and take up the slack.

2 Pick up two 8°s and one 11°. Ladder these to the last two 8°s added in the initial ring, so the 11°s are on the same side.

3 Pick up one 11° and two 8°s. Ladder these beads to the last two 8°s added in the previous step.

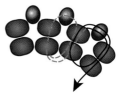

4 Repeat steps 2 and 3 six more times until you have 16 pairs of 8°s. Join the first pair to the last pair by stitching through the first pair of 8°s added, picking up one 11°, and stitching through the last pair of 8°s added in a circular thread path, laddering the two pairs together. Weave through the first pair of 8°s, the first 11°, and the second pair of 8°s so your thread is emerging on the inside of the ring.

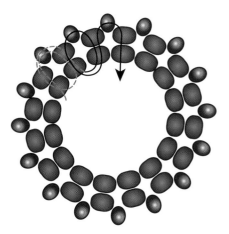

BEZEL BACK

5 Stitch one row of 11°s in tubular herringbone stitch from off the inner row of 8°s, stepping up at the end of the round to exit the first 11° added.

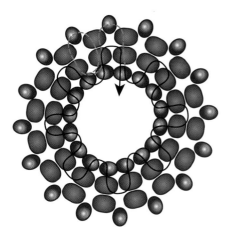

6 Add a single 13° atop each ladder in herringbone stitch. At the end of the round, stitch down through the 8°s to the outside of the ring, then through the nearest 11° and the following 8°, heading toward the inside of the ring.

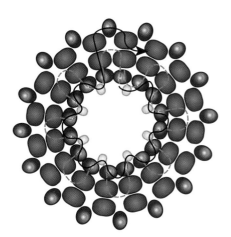

BEZEL FRONT

7 Add one round of 8°s in tubular herringbone stitch, using the outer ring of 8°s as the base.

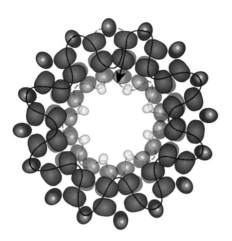

8 Add two rounds of 11°s in tubular herringbone—one round off the 8°s added in step 7 and one round off the 11°s just added.

9 Place a cabochon in the bezel. Add a single 13° atop each ladder in herringbone stitch, pulling your thread tight after each stitch.

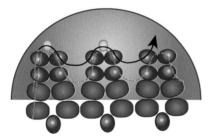

10 Each bezel will add just less than 1 inch (2.5 cm) to the finished length of the bracelet. The closure will not add any additional length. Repeat steps 1–9 to create as many bezels as you need to achieve the desired bracelet length. The bracelet shown has seven bezels.

JOINING BEZELS

11 Needle up the hanging thread on one of the bezels. Stitch through the 8°s in the bezel, bringing your thread out of the outer ring of 8°s, then the nearest 11°. Pick up one fire-polished round. Stitch through an 11° on the outer edge of the next bezel, then back through the fire-polished round and into the other side of the first 11°.

Weave through the 8°s on the outer edge and bring your thread out of the third 11° on the edge from the first. Pick up one fire-polished round, then stitch through the 11° three from the first on the next bezel, back through the fire-polished round, and into the other side of the first 11°. Repeat the thread path at least one more time to reinforce the connection.

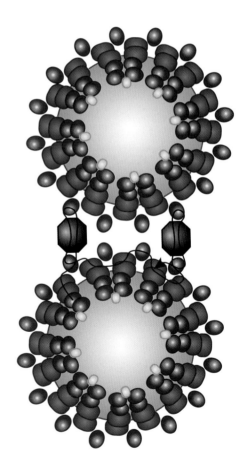

12 Secure your thread in one of the bezels and trim it. Repeat step 11 to join the remaining bezels to the first two. Leave the thread hanging on each end bezel, but weave in and trim the threads hanging on all of the inner bezels.

CLOSURE
13 Needle up the hanging thread on one end bezel. Bring the thread out of the 8° in the second from outer round on the front side of the bezel, directly opposite the attachment point to the next bezel. Pick up one 11°, the rondelle, and one 11°. Skip the last 11°, stitch back through the rondelle and the next 11°, then into the 8° in the bezel. Repeat this thread path several times to reinforce, then secure your thread in the beadwork and trim it.

14 Needle up the hanging thread on the other end bezel. Bring your thread out of an 8° in the second from outer round, one from the point directly opposite the attachment point to the next bezel. Pick up thirteen 11°s and stitch into the 8° in the second from outer round on the other side of the point directly opposite the attachment point to the next bezel, forming a loop. Repeat this thread path as many times as the bead holes will allow to reinforce, then weave your thread into the beadwork, secure it, and trim it.

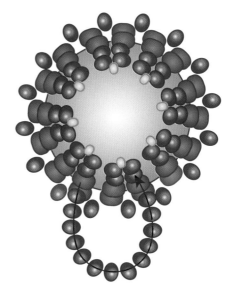

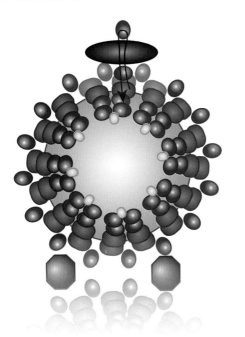

Back

athena necklace

This necklace is named after the Greek goddess who represents many virtues, including wisdom, beauty, and arts and crafts. The colors in this necklace remind me of the blue of the Mediterranean and the warm gold tones in Greek mythological paintings.

YOU'LL NEED

Size 8° silk bronze iris round seed beads, 13 g

Size 11° round seed beads:

A, silk light gold, 9 g

B, silk bronze iris, 5 g

Amazonite puffed coin bead, 5 x 25 mm

3 amazonite puffed coin beads, 5 x 16 mm

Size 12 beading needles

Gold beading thread

Scissors

Work surface

TECHNIQUES

Ladder Stitch or Ndebele Start with Varying Bead Sizes

Two-Ladder Tubular Herringbone Stitch

Single-Ladder Herringbone Stitch

Faux Bezel

DIMENSIONS

20 inches (50.8 cm) long

DIFFICULTY LEVEL

Intermediate

OVERVIEW

You'll create the centerpiece, side pieces, chain, and closure of this necklace separately, then assemble them together at the end. Bead the majority of the necklace in two-ladder tubular herringbone stitch.

CENTERPIECE

1 Needle up one wingspan of thread and create a two-ladder tubular herringbone base using either technique, with 8°s on one ladder and As on the other. Leave a 6-inch (12.5 cm) tail to secure in the beadwork later.

2 Stitch 48 rows total, adding only 8°s to the 8° ladder and As to the A ladder. The tube will curve after 12 rows. Zip row 48 to row 1 as the next row you'll pick up to continue the two-ladder herringbone stitch. This will keep the thread path consistent.

3 Continuing to work in the same direction, bring your thread out of an 8° and pick up one A. Stitch into the closest A in the next row, then through five more As. Pick up one A and stitch through the closest 8° in the next row, then through five more 8°s. Continuing in the same manner, pick up one A, then stitch through six As; pick up one 11°, then stitch through six 8°s. Pick up one A.

4 Stitch through the closest A in the next row, the adjacent 8°, and the A you just added.

5 Pick up a group of six As and stitch through the fourth A added to the ring, from the inside of the ring to the outside. Pick up three As and stitch back through the fourth A, creating a 3-bead picot. Repeat to add a group of six As and 3-bead picots two more times. Pick up six As. Stitch through the first A added to the ring, then through an 8° and an A, bringing your thread out of the inside of the ring.

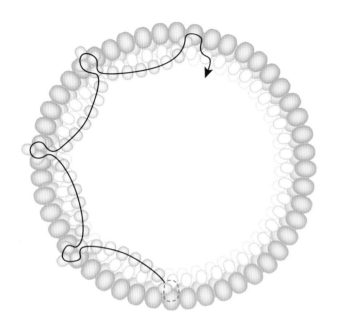

6 Pick up the 25-mm amazonite puffed coin and stitch through the other side of the ring. Weave through two As, then stitch back through the coin and into the other side of the ring. Repeat this thread path several times to reinforce, then secure your thread in the beadwork and trim it.

SIDE PIECES

1 Needle up a wingspan of thread and start a two-ladder herringbone base as you did for the centerpiece, with 8°s on one ladder and As on the other. Leave a 14-inch (35.6 cm) tail. Stitch 23 rows, adding 8°s to the 8° ladder and As to the A ladder.

2 Reverse the beads you're adding to each ladder; begin adding pairs of As to the 8° ladder and 8°s to the A ladder. This section of the tube will curve in the opposite direction of the first. Stitch a total of 27 rows in this manner. Bringing your thread out of an 8° in the last row, switch to single-ladder herringbone stitch. Add four pairs of 8°s in single-ladder herringbone stitch to the 8° ladder. Leave your thread hanging.

Needle up your 14-inch (35.6 cm) tail at the beginning of the tube. Bring your thread out of an 8° in the end row and add two pairs of 8°s in single ladder herringbone stitch to the 8° ladder. Then add one final 8° to the end of the ladder.

3 With the current working thread, weave down through the beadwork and bring your thread out of an A in the sixth row. Pick up a 16-mm amazonite puffed coin and stitch across the tube, inserting your needle between the 23rd and 24th rows, where the tube changes. Curl the other end of the tube so you can stitch through the tube between the 49th and 50th rows. Reinforce the connection in the reverse direction by stitching through the tube in a different spot, the first half of the tube again, and the amazonite puffed coin; secure your thread in the beadwork and trim it.

Needle up the other thread and use it to tack the end of the single ladder to the inside of the curved tube.

4 Weave in a new 18-inch (45.7 cm) piece of thread near the first row of the tube. Bring it out of an A in the fourth row so you are working from the start of the tube toward the end. Pick up five As and stitch through the A in the eighth row on the same side of the A ladder. Pick up seven As and stitch through the A in the 15th row on the same side of the A ladder. Pick up nine As and stitch through the A in the 23rd row on the same side of the A ladder. Secure your thread in the beadwork and trim it.

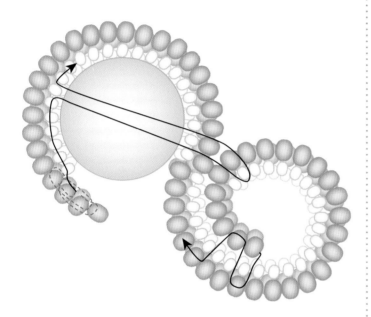

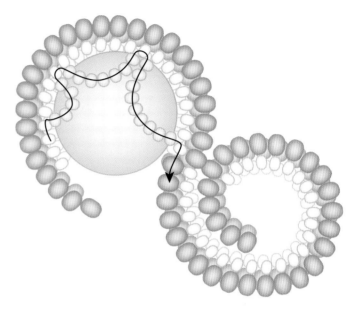

5 Create a second side piece that is a mirror image of the first. Accomplish this after completing the main portion of the tube and additional single-ladder rows by stitching the embellishments (shown in the illustration beneath Rows 82–117) to the As on the other side of the two-ladder herringbone tube.

CHAIN

Rows 1–17: Needle up a wingspan of thread and start a two-ladder tubular herringbone base with 8°s on one ladder and As on the other, leaving a 12-inch (30.5 cm) tail. Add a total of 17 rows with 8°s on the 8° ladder and As on the A ladder.

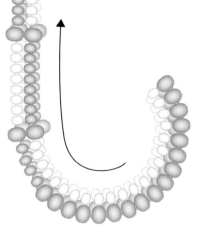

Rows 18–21: Add four rows with Bs on the 8° ladder and As on the 8° ladder.

Row 22: Add 8°s on both ladders.

Rows 23–30: Add As on the 8° ladder and Bs on the A ladder.

Row 31: Add 8°s on both ladders.

Rows 32–47: Add Bs on the 8° ladder and As on the A ladder.

Row 48: Add 8°s on both ladders.

Rows 49–80: Add As on the 8° ladder and Bs on the A ladder.

Row 81: Add 8°s on both ladders.

Rows 82–117: Add Bs on the 8° ladder and As on the A ladder.

For a 20-inch (50.8 cm) necklace, stitch up to the 117th row.

For additional length, add eight rows for each inch (2.5 cm).

Last Row: Add 8°s on both ladders. Leave the thread hanging if you have at least 18 inches (45.7 cm).

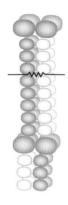

Pick up the hanging thread at the beginning of the chain. Bring it out of an 8° in the first row. Switch to singe-ladder herringbone stitch and add one pair of 8°s to the 8° ladder. Add one 8° to the end of the ladder.

Create a second chain identical to the first for the other side of the necklace.

2 Bring your thread out of an A in the inner ring. Pick up four As, one 8°, and *four As, then stitch through the A eight down from the one from which your thread last emerged. Stitch back through the last four As, then pick up one 8° and repeat from * two more times. Pick up one 8° and stitch down through the first four As you picked up.

Repeat all the thread paths through the beads you just added to reinforce the connections. Secure your thread in the beadwork and trim it.

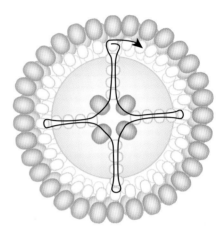

CLOSURE

1 Start a two-ladder herringbone stitch base with As on one ladder and 8°s on the other ladder. Stitch 32 rows, then join the end to the beginning with the same join you used in the centerpiece. Stitch a 16-mm amazonite puffed coin bead in the center of the ring.

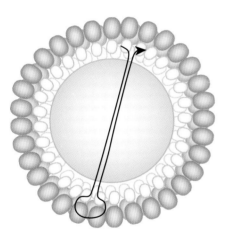

3 Pick up the hanging thread on the end of the neck chain or start a new thread and bring it out of an 8° on the end. Add 42 rows of Bs in single-ladder herringbone stitch onto the 8° ladder.

4 Stitch the end of the ladder to the other ladder on the end of the neck chain as though the end pair of 8°s is the next pair you'll pick up. Secure your thread in the beadwork and trim it.

5 Pick up the hanging thread on the other neck chain end, or start a new thread close to the end and bring it out of an 8°. Pick up 13 Bs, then stitch through three of the 8°s on the back side of the toggle button. Pick up 13 Bs, then stitch into a different 8° on the end of the neck chain. Repeat the thread path several times to reinforce the connection, then secure your thread in the beadwork and trim it.

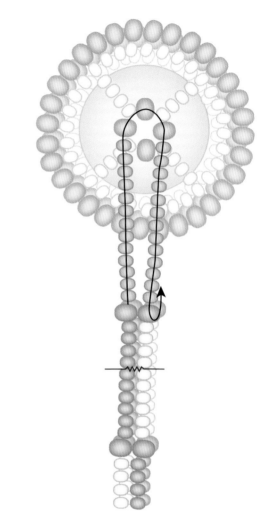

ASSEMBLE

When you assemble the necklace, tack the pieces together as if you are sewing clothing, keeping your stitches tight and as invisible as possible. You can either stitch back and forth through each tube, without going through beads, or stitch back and forth through adjacent beads in each piece.

To attach the chain to the side piece, tack the chain near the ninth bead from the start to the side piece near the ninth bead from the start. To attach the side piece to the centerpiece, tack the side piece near the 16th bead from the end to the centerpiece near the ninth bead from the top center.

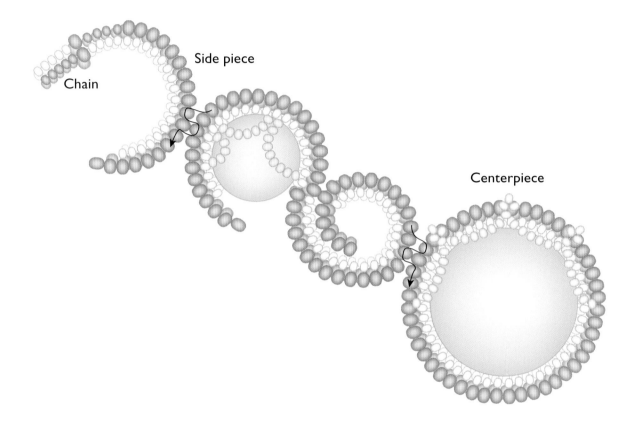

Chain

Side piece

Centerpiece

da vinci earrings

Rivolis are captured in bezels created with tubular herringbone stitch. Each bezel is then embellished heavily to create an intricate, encrusted look. The name of the earrings was inspired by their rustic, antique look.

YOU'LL NEED

Size 8° matte raku plum/bronze iris seed beads, 2 g

Size 11° round seed beads:

    A, metallic bronze, 2 g

    B, metallic light blue nickel-plated, 1 g

Size 15° round seed beads:

    C, metallic bronze, 1 g

    D, matte raku plum/blue iris, 1 g

2 celadon crystal rivolis, 14 mm

16 aqua/celadon crystal bicones, 4 mm

2 gold-plated ear wires

Size 12 beading needles

Gray beading thread

Scissors

Work surface

TECHNIQUES

Ladder Stitch

Tubular Herringbone Stitch

DIMENSIONS

1⁵/₈ inches (4.1 cm) long

DIFFICULTY LEVEL

Advanced

OVERVIEW

You'll create the bezel for the rivoli, embellish it with several different beads for an opulent look, and add the ear wire at the very end.

BASE

1 Needle up a wingspan of thread. Leaving just enough of a tail to weave into the beadwork later and secure, pick up two 8°s, one A, and two 8°s. Pass through all the beads again and take up the slack.

2 Pick up two 8°s and one A. Ladder these to the last two 8°s exited from the initial ring, so the As are on the same side.

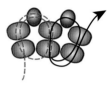

3 Pick up one A and two 8°s. Ladder these beads to the last two 8°s exited from the previous pair of 8°s.

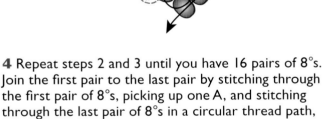

4 Repeat steps 2 and 3 until you have 16 pairs of 8°s. Join the first pair to the last pair by stitching through the first pair of 8°s, picking up one A, and stitching through the last pair of 8°s in a circular thread path, laddering the two pairs together. Weave through the first pair of 8°s, the first A, and the second pair of 8°s so your thread is emerging on the inside of the ring.

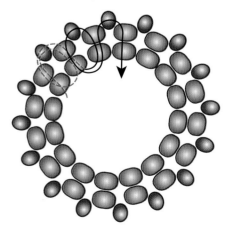

BEZEL BACK

5 Stitch one row of As in tubular herringbone stitch from the inner row of 8°s, stepping up at the end of the round.

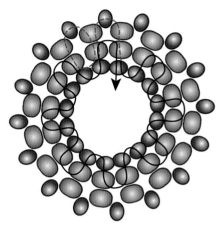

6 Add a single C atop each ladder in herringbone stitch. At the end of the round, stitch down through the 8°s to the outside of the ring, the nearest A, and the adjacent 8°, heading toward the inside of the ring.

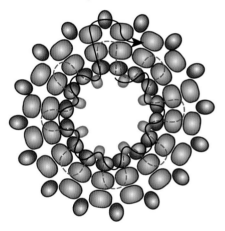

BEZEL FRONT

7 Working counterclockwise, add one round of 8°s in tubular herringbone stitch, using the outer ring of 8°s as the base.

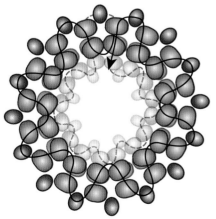

8 Add one round of As in tubular herringbone stitch.

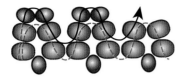

9 Place the rivoli in the bezel. Add a single C atop each ladder in herringbone stitch, pulling your thread tight after each stitch. Repeat the thread path through the round, pulling each stitch tight.

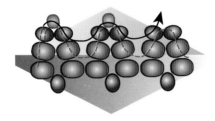

EMBELLISHMENT

10 Stitch through to exit the adjacent 8° added in step 7. Pick up one C, one bicone, and one C. Stitch up through the first 8° in the second row of the next ladder, heading in toward the center of the bezel. Pick up one B. Stitch out through the second 8° in the second row of the ladder. Repeat this step all around the bezel, then bring your thread out of the edge row of 8°s and the nearest A.

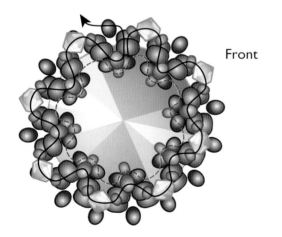

Front

FINISH

11 Pick up two Ds and stitch through the next A on the edge of the bezel. Repeat 14 times. Pick up five Ds and the bottom loop of the ear wire, then stitch through the next A. Repeat the thread path through all of the Ds and the ear wire loop at least one more time to reinforce.

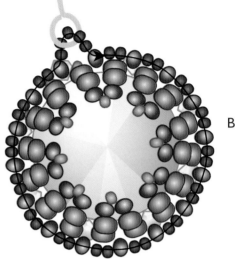

Back

Repeat all steps to make a second earring.

sinusoidal
necklace

This necklace takes its
name from a graphical
representation of the
relationship between
a triangle's angle
and two of its sides.
This relationship is a
critical tool in physics,
engineering, and
mathematics.
Did I mention I'm a
science geek?

YOU'LL NEED

Size 8° round seed beads:

A, silk dark bronze iris, 17 g

B, transparent matte light smoked topaz AB, 9 g

Size 11° round seed beads:

C, silk light gold, 8 g

D, silk dark bronze iris, 1 g

Size 15° metallic purple gold iris round seed beads, 3 g

Size 15° metallic bronze charlotte seed beads, 1 g

Size 11° transparent brown gold luster cylinder beads, 2 g

Tabac crystal stone, 22 x 30 mm

Purple haze crystal rivoli, 18 mm

Champagne Czech fire-polished rounds, 8 mm*

Light Colorado topaz AB crystal bicones, 4 mm*

Smoke topaz AB crystal bicones, 3 mm*

Size 6° silk gold iris round seed beads, 4 g

Size 12 and 13 beading needles

Polyethylene or other strong beading thread

Scissors

Work surface

* See the box to the right.

• •

TECHNIQUES

Ndebele Start with Varying Bead Sizes

Single-Ladder Herringbone Stitch

Two-Ladder Tubular Herringbone Stitch

Bezeled Stones

Flat Peyote Stitch

• •

DIMENSIONS

15 inches (38.1 cm) long

• •

DIFFICULTY LEVEL

Advanced

The number of beads to get depends on how long you want to make the necklace. Use the chart below to determine how many you need.

Necklace Length	# of 8-mm fire-polished rounds	# of 4-mm bicones	# of 3-mm bicones	# of repeats per side
13 inches (33 cm)	19	25	105	4½
16 inches (40.6 cm)	21	27	117	5
19 inches (48.3 cm)	23	27	127	5½
22 inches (55.9 cm)	25	29	139	6
25 inches (63.5 cm)	27	29	149	6½
28 inches (71.1 cm)	29	31	161	7

OVERVIEW

This necklace is composed of several different components created separately, then stitched together. You'll make the two neckband halves using two-ladder tubular herringbone stitch. You'll bezel the crystal stones with tubular peyote stitch and add embellishments, then create the toggle bar with flat peyote stitch and the toggle ring with two-ladder tubular herringbone stitch.

Finally, you'll connect bezels to the neckband, attach the closure, and add embellishments to the centerpiece and outer edges of the neckband. Use your size 12 needle for most of the project.

NECKBAND

You'll create the first half of the neckband from front to back and repeat to create the second half of the neckband from front to back as well, each time saving a long tail to add a detail of single-ladder herringbone stitch at the beginning.

Rows 1–3: Needle up a wingspan of thread onto your size 12 needle and start a two-ladder tube of herringbone stitch with the Ndebele method (page 60) using A on ladder 1 and C on ladder 2; leave an 18-inch (45.7 cm) tail.

Note: You'll always step up through ladder 1 when doing this stitch for this necklace. If you lose your place, look for your tail thread—it will be emerging from the bottom of ladder 1.

Rows 4–5: Stitch these rows using A on ladder 1 and C on ladder 2.

Rows 6–9: Add B on ladder 1 and C on ladder 2.

Rows 10–14: Add A on ladder 1 and C on ladder 2. You'll now switch the beads you're adding to each ladder, and start adding As onto ladder 2 and Cs onto ladder 1.

Rows 15–19: Add C on ladder 1 and A on ladder 2.

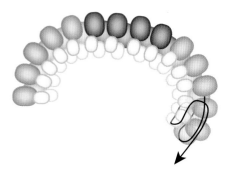

Rows 20–25: Add C on ladder 1 and B on ladder 2.

Rows 26–30: Add C on ladder 1 and A on ladder 2.

"Up wave" on inside of neck band

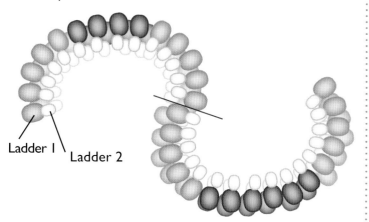

Ladder 1   Ladder 2

"Down wave" on outside of neck band

You've just finished one complete repeat. Continue stitching the neckband half, stitching repeats of rows 1 to 30, paying close attention to which beads you add to which ladder. Five repeats on each side will give you a necklace 16 inches (40.6 cm) long when finished. One

extra repeat on each side adds just over 3 inches (7.6 cm) to the necklace—1½ inches (3.8 cm) per side. (See the chart on page 114 to find out how many repeats to make for your desired necklace length.)

When you've finished creating repeats, leave your hanging thread for later. Needle up your tail thread, and work from the start of the neckband half.

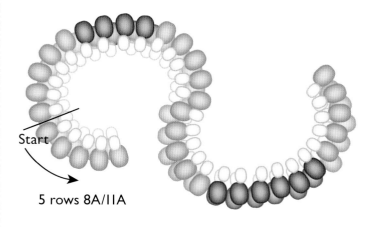

Start

5 rows 8A/11A

Add five extra rows using A on ladder 1 and C on ladder 2.

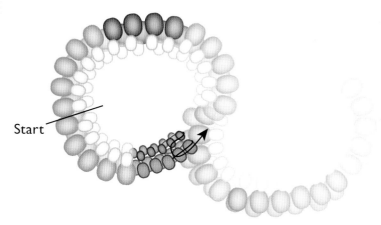

Start

Add five rows using D on ladder 1 and 15° rounds on ladder 2.

Switch to single-ladder herringbone stitch after the fifth row. Add three rows of single-ladder herringbone stitch using D and one row of single-ladder herringbone stitch using 15° rounds.

Secure your thread in the beadwork and trim it. Repeat to create the second neckband.

Top view

OVAL BEZEL

Needle up a wingspan of thread onto your size 13 needle. Pick up 64 cylinder beads and center them on your thread so you have an equal length of thread on each side. ***Note:*** If the cylinder beads are a little on the large side, try the bezel with 62. Stitch through the first few beads again to form a loop. Be sure to step up at the end of each row.

- Add two rounds of cylinder beads in tubular peyote stitch.

- Add two rounds of 15° rounds and one round of 15° charlottes.

- Depending on how tight or loose your beadwork is, you may have to add an extra round of 15° charlottes. Leave the thread hanging for embellishment.

Needle up your tail thread (black dot). Put your stone in the bezel, front side down, and hold in place while you stitch two rounds of 15° rounds and one round of 15° charlottes. Again, depending on your thread tension, you may need to add an extra round of 15° charlottes. Leave the thread hanging for embellishment.

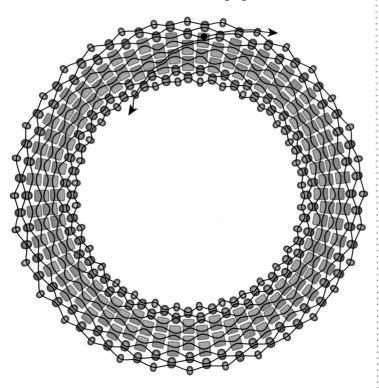

RIVOLI BEZEL

Needle up a wingspan of thread onto your size 13 needle. Center 46 cylinders on the thread. Go through the first few beads again to form a loop. Stitch one round of cylinders, two rounds of 15° rounds, and one round of 15° charlottes, making sure you step up at the end of each row.

Needle up your tail thread. Stitch one round of 15° rounds, then put your rivoli in the bezel, front side down. Stitch another round of 15° rounds, then one round of 15° charlottes. Depending on your thread tension, you may need to add one more round of 15° charlottes to hold the stone securely in place; use your judgment. Leave the threads hanging for embellishment.

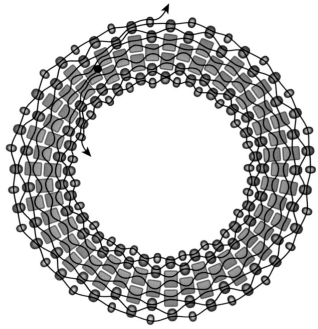

CENTERPIECE
You'll join and embellish the two crystal bezels.

Weave one of your hanging threads on your rivoli bezel to the center round of cylinders. Pick up one 8-mm fire-polished bead, one 4-mm bicone, and one 15° round. Go back through the bicone and round, then through the next cylinder, one cylinder in an adjacent row, and the next cylinder.

Add seven 4-mm bicones anchored with 15° rounds to the center round of cylinder beads, then add one 3-mm bicone anchored with a 15° round. Stitch through one cylinder in an adjacent row and the next cylinder. Add cylinders in peyote stitch in the next two spaces. Stitch through one cylinder in an adjacent row and the next cylinder, then repeat the embellishment of the 3-mm bicone and seven 4-mm bicones. Secure your thread in the beadwork and trim it.

If you have enough length, use the same hanging thread to add five 3-mm bicones anchored with 15° rounds to the center of the top of the oval bezel, opposite the rivoli bezel.

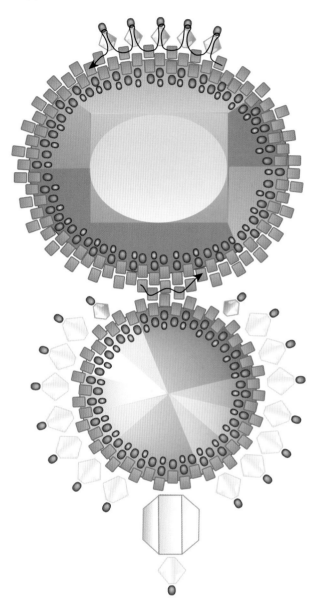

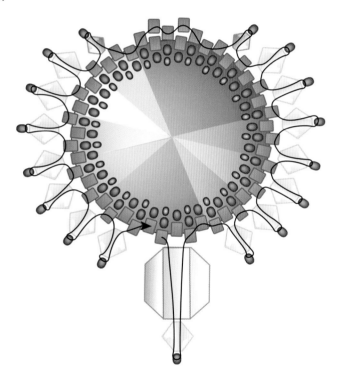

Use one of the hanging threads on the oval bezel to add the two cylinders on top of the rivoli bezel in peyote stitch to the center round of cylinders.

Leave the longest hanging thread for adding the neckband; secure the shorter thread in the beadwork and trim it.

TOGGLE BAR

Needle up 1 yard (91.4 cm) of thread onto your size 12 needle. Pick up twelve Cs. Stitch eight rows of flat peyote stitch using Cs from off this initial line for a total of 10 rows.

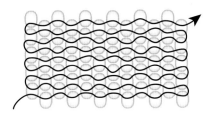

Zip the peyote strip into a tube by weaving alternately through beads in the first and last rows. Then stitch into the middle of the tube.

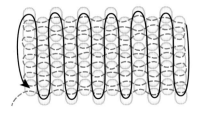

Bring your thread out of the other end of the tube. Pick up one 4-mm bicone and one 15° round. Stitch back through the bicone and through the tube to the other end. Pick up one 4-mm bicone and one 15° round. Stitch back through the bicone and into the tube. Repeat the thread path through these embellishments for added strength, then secure your thread in the beadwork and trim it.

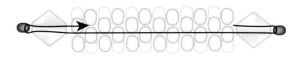

TOGGLE LOOP

Rows 1–3: Needle up a half wingspan of thread. Start a two-ladder tubular herringbone base using the Ndebele method (page 50), with As on ladder 1 and Cs on ladder 2.

Rows 4–5: Add As on ladder 1 and Cs on ladder 2.

Rows 6–9: Add Bs on ladder 1 and Cs on ladder 2.

Rows 10–14: Add As on ladder 1 and Cs on ladder 2.

Rows 15–18: Add Bs on ladder 1 and Cs on ladder 2.

Join the last row to the first row by picking up the beads in the first row as if you're adding them to row 19, and complete the row by stepping up. Secure your thread in the beadwork and trim it.

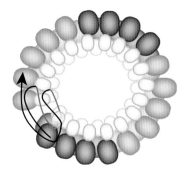

ASSEMBLE

You'll connect the centerpiece to the neckband halves, add 8-mm fire-polished beads between the waves, and attach the toggle bar and toggle loop to the ends of the necklace.

Needle up the hanging thread on the oval bezel. Weave through the bezel until your thread is emerging from roughly the 2 o'clock position.

Position one of the neckband halves with the start close to where the thread is emerging from the oval bezel. Position one 8-mm fire-polished bead in the rounded end of the neckband and wrap the end of the neckband around the 8-mm bead so there's little space between the neckband and the bead.

Holding this assembly in place, ladder two beads in the center round of the bezel to two As on the outside of the herringbone tube. Ladder two beads in the round below to the two As on the other side of the ladder as well for added stability.

Stitch directly through the herringbone tube, through the 8-mm fire-polished bead, through the end of the herringbone tube, then through the herringbone tube right at the junction where you first flipped the order of the beads in the ladders.

1 Pick up one 6°, one 8-mm fire-polished bead, and one 6°. Stitch directly through the herringbone tube at the next junction where the ladders flip.

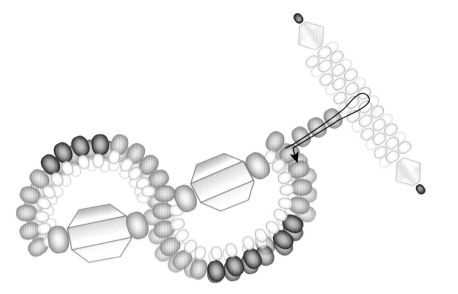

2 Continue adding these 6°s and 8-mm fire-polished beads between the junctions of the tube where the ladders flip, until you reach the end of the neckband half.

Pick up seven As and stitch into the middle of the toggle bar, then reverse direction, making sure you catch some thread or beads, and stitch back through the As and into the neckband. If you need extra incremental length, you can add more As here.

3 Repeat the thread path between the toggle bar and the oval bezel, through all of the 8-mm fire-polished beads and 6°s, at least twice more to reinforce the connections. When you're finished, secure your thread in the beadwork and trim it.

Assemble the second half of the necklace exactly like the first, but use three As to add the toggle loop at the end. If you need extra incremental length, you can add more As here. Repeat the thread path, attaching the loop to the necklace several times, then secure your thread in the beadwork and trim it.

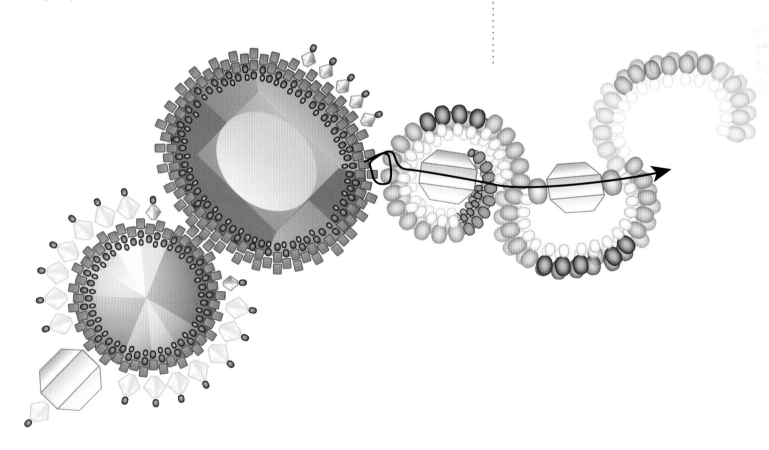

gallery

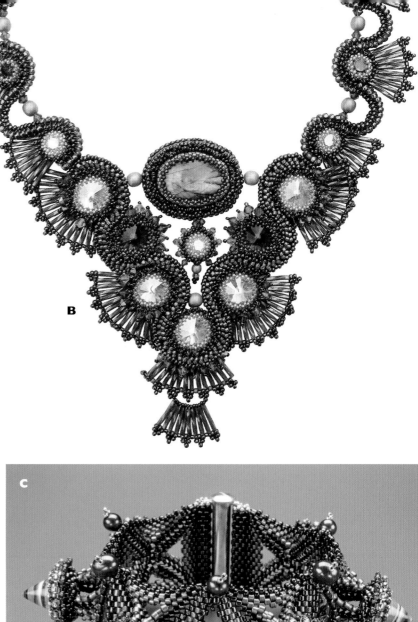

A MARCIA DECOSTER
Aurelia, 2010
2 x 3 x 13 cm
Seed beads, crystals
PHOTO BY ARTIST

B MIRIAM SHIMON
Jewel of Amun, 2010
27 x 17 x 12 cm
Seed beads, rivolis; herringbone stitch,
peyote stitch
PHOTO BY ARTIST

C LAURA MCCABE
Carnival Eiffel Tower Bracelet, 2010
2.5 x 17 x 2.5 cm
Custom-cut rainbow calsilica points,
seed beads, freshwater pearls, 14-karat
gold clasp; herringbone stitch,
peyote stitch
PHOTO BY MELINDA HOLDEN

D MIRIAM SHIMON
La Prima Vera, 2011
32 x 18 x 13 cm
Rivolis, bugle beads, seed beads;
herringbone stitch, peyote stitch
PHOTO BY ARTIST

D

E LESLIE FRAZIER
Autumn Dreams, 2007
7.6 × 7.6 × 1.3 cm
Seed beads, cylinder beads, fire-polished beads; herringbone stitch, peyote stitch, right angle weave
PHOTO BY TOM FRAZIER

F HUIB PETERSEN
Dragonfly on Calla Lily, 1996
66 cm long; flower, 1.9 cm; dragonfly, 6.3 × 5.1 cm
Seed beads, onyx beads; herringbone stitch, peyote stitch
PHOTO BY ARTIST

G LAURA MCCABE
Treasure Necklace, 2010
Box, 2.5 × 2.5 × 2 cm each
Crystal stones, crystals, freshwater pearls, seed beads; herringbone stitch, peyote stitch
PHOTOS BY MELINDA HOLDEN

H HUIB PETERSEN
Art Nouveau Sweet Pea, 2010
Seed beads, crystals; diagonal peyote stitch, herringbone stitch
PHOTO BY ARTIST

A

Matrimonial Headdress, 2009
23 x 18 cm at widest point,
not including drops
Seed beads, crystal beads, glass pearls,
freshwater pearls, nonwoven stitching
base, felt, wire, wire mesh, plastic mesh,
ribbon, barrette finding
PHOTO BY ARTIST

B

Fresh Tendrils, 2011
46 cm
Seed beads, crystal beads, freshwater
pearls; two-ladder tubular herringbone
stitch, stringing, peyote stitch
PHOTO BY ARTIST

C

Inexplicably Ndebele, 2009
64 cm
Seed beads, crystal beads, glass beads;
two-ladder tubular herringbone stitch,
spiral herringbone stitch
PHOTO BY ARTIST

APPENDIX:
SEED BEADS USED IN PROJECTS

In case you want to exactly replicate a project as it's pictured in this book, this list tells you what brand and color of bead I used.

Athena Necklace
8°: Czech 01610
A: Czech 01710
B: Czech 01610

Beaded Capsule Pendant
8°: Czech 01630
11°: Czech 01610
15°: Miyuki 462
A: Toho 421
B: Toho 457

Braided Bracelet
A: Czech 01770
B: Czech 68304
C: Toho 558PF

Center of Gravity Earrings
A: Toho 995
B: Toho 558F
C: Czech 01710
15°: Toho 995

Component Bracelet
11° cylinder: Toho 714
11°: Toho 560
15°: Toho 710

Da Vinci Earrings
A: Toho 221
B: Toho 512
8°: Toho 514
C: Toho 221
D: Toho 704

Descending Scales Pendant
8°: Toho 514F
11°: Czech 01610
15°: Miyuki 462

Earth Mother Earrings
3-mm cube: Miyuki 2035
10° cylinder: Miyuki 380
11° cylinder: Toho Aiko 1506
8°: Toho 151
15°: Toho 279

Fern Earrings
A: Czech 59148
B: Czech 59145
8°: Czech 01630
15°: Miyuki 462

Floral Ring
8°: Toho 926
11°: Toho 557PF

Hodgepodge Bracelet
A: Czech 07122M
B: Czech 01700
C: Czech 23980

Lacy Wrap Choker
A: Miyuki 256BF
B: Toho 740M
C: Toho 998
D: Miyuki 514D

Opulent Beaded Bead
11°: Czech 23560
A: Toho 421
B: Toho 457

Pod Earrings
A: Toho 999
B: Toho 710
11° cylinder: Toho 714

Poseidon's Gem Bracelet
15°: Toho F463W
11° cylinder: Aiko 1700
11°: Toho 369
8°: Toho 702
6°: Toho Y504

Quartets Bracelet
8°: Czech 01700

Sinusoidal Necklace
11° cylinder: Miyuki 115
A: Czech 01630 or 01640
B: Czech 11110*
C: Czech 01710
D: Czech 01610
15°: Miyuki 462
6°: Czech 01620
*Note: Difficult to find! A good substitute is Miyuki 134FR.

Spellbound Bracelet
8°: Toho 401F
11°: Toho Y541
13°: Czech 18581spg

Spindle Earrings
15°: Toho 222
11°: Czech 01770
8°: Miyuki 641

Starry Night Necklace
11°: Czech 38649
15°: Toho 713

Sweet Sets Necklace
15°: Toho 995
11° cylinder: Toho Aiko 144
11°: Toho 557

Transcription Bracelet
11°: Matsuno 648
6°: Toho 703
15° : Toho 998
Magatama: Toho 85M

Trumpet Lily Earrings
8°: Toho 513F
11°: Czech 01710
15°: Toho 994

Two-Ladder Tennis Bracelet
8°: Miyuki 462
11°: Toho 221

Victorian Elegance Necklace
A: Miyuki 342
B: Czech 01610
C: Czech 01630
11°: Czech 01710
15°: Toho 222
Magatama: Toho 421

Willow Lariat
13°: Czech 18304

ACKNOWLEDGMENTS

I could never have tackled this book without my wonderful editor, Nathalie Mornu, who worked tirelessly to get this book in order and was exceptionally tolerant of my unusual schedule.

Rachel Nelson-Smith, who I met for the first time during this project, was a perfect match as technical editor. Her easygoing style was a welcome approach to what could have been a stressful process. It was an honor to work with such an inspiring and accomplished beader.

It's important I thank those who got me started in this field. Ann Benson took me on as a recent college graduate needing a job and taught me more about beading, writing directions, and this business than I ever could have dreamed. Renee Frost and Kate Branstetter, who sat with me and taught me different beading techniques, gave me constant love and encouragement. They boosted my confidence in my work, which allowed me to put myself out into the world, giving my career a real chance.

This book and my career in beading wouldn't exist without the constant moral support of a few beaders who welcomed me into the beading realm and have been incredibly helpful as I've worked to find my creative voice. It has been a dream to get so much encouragement and advice from Sherry Serafini, Diane Hyde, and Laura McCabe. They are a constant source of inspiration. This book certainly wouldn't have been possible without help from Laura McCabe, who first taught me tubular herringbone stitch and the Ndebele start. I've learned many of the other techniques in this book from her as well.

Finally, I'd like to thank my family, which has allowed me the space to undertake this task and offered unwavering support during the long hours I put into writing the book and stitching its projects. My mother, father, and Jane all babysat my son so that I could squeeze out the extra hours I needed. Jack played quietly for as long as he possibly could so that I could work. And the biggest thanks go to my incredible husband, Shippee, who has tolerated my absence, given an extra hand with Jack and around the house, and been morally supportive of each and every one of my creative endeavors, no matter how lengthy or stressful or trying they've been. I couldn't have accomplished this book or started my career without him.

PHOTO BY AUTHOR

ABOUT MELISSA GRAKOWSKY

I fell in love with beading in 2007. I had just finished dual bachelor's degrees in art and physics at the University of Connecticut and was home with a new baby. A friend surfing the Internet showed me Laura McCabe's otherworldly, surreal beadwork designs, and I felt I'd fallen into a whole new world! I quickly became a regular customer at a local bead store and got absolutely obsessed. Working with seed beads provided the intensely focused creative outlet I dearly needed, in a new medium that matched my new lifestyle perfectly.

Since beginning my beading career, I've won numerous prizes for my jewelry designs and elaborate beaded masks, which are one of my favorite things to stitch. These awards include Grand Prize in Fire Mountain Gems and Beads' 2010 polymer clay contest, Bead Star's 2010 top prize in glass beads, and third place in the 2009 Bead Dreams objects and accessories category. I regularly teach workshops nationally and internationally and love sharing with students as well as learning from them. I enjoy creating sculptural forms using different sizes of seed beads and am currently infatuated with herringbone stitch. I hope this book helps you, too, fall in love with this incredibly versatile stitch!

INDEX

GALLERY CONTRIBUTORS

ADDITIONAL PHOTO CREDITS

All images appear on page 5.
Brick pavement
http://en.wikipedia.org/wiki/Herringbone_pattern
Basketry
© iStockphoto/phleum
Tweed
© iStockphoto/lucentius